The
CHATTOOGA
Wild and Scenic River

Third Edition

by Brian A. Boyd

The Chattooga Wild and Scenic River
Third Edition

Published and Distributed by
Fern Creek Press
P.O. Box 1322
Clayton, GA 30525
(706) 782-5379

Copyright 1998 © Fern Creek Press

All rights reserved. No portion of this book may be reproduced in any form or by any means without the prior written permission of Brian Boyd and Fern Creek Press, excepting brief quotes used in connection with reviews, written specifically for inclusion in a magazine or newspaper.

Printed in the United States of America
by J & M Printing Co., Clayton, GA

1st printing 1990
2nd printing 1992
3rd printing 1995
4th printing 1998

First Edition ISBN 0-9625737-0-1
Second Edition ISBN 0-9625737-4-4
Third Edition ISBN 0-9625737-9-5

The author and publisher of this guidebook assume no responsibility for any loss of property, accident, injury or death sustained while visiting any of the locations described herein. Both natural and man-made changes occur which may make descriptions in this publication obsolete or erroneous. The very nature of this area makes these locations potentially dangerous to visit and explore. Please use caution and good common sense when in the wild. Please follow all Forest Service rules and regulations when visiting the Chattooga Wild and Scenic River.

Acknowledgments
Thank you to Greg Borgen of the Andrew Pickens Ranger District, U.S. Forest Service for providing updated information on river usage. The author also wishes to acknowledge the excellent interpretive guide *The Chattooga Sourcebook* by William Clay. This authoritative compilation proved to be an invaluable resource for localized information on Chattooga history, geography, flora, fauna and climate.

Table of Contents

Chapter One - Introduction
Introduction 2
Geography and Topography 4
Chattooga Flora 5
Chattooga Fauna 8
Weather and Climate 11
Safety Considerations 12
Brief Historical Highlights 14

Chapter Two - The Chattooga Headwaters
Headwaters Map 18
Headwaters Overview 19
Whiteside Mountain Trail 20
Cashiers Sliding Rock 21
Chattooga Cliffs Trail 22
Bull Pen Bridge Loop Trail 23
Ellicott Rock Wilderness 25
Bad Creek Trail 27
Ellicott Rock Trail 28
Sloan Bridge Trail 29
East Fork Trail 30
Fish Hatchery & Chattooga Picnic Area 31
Burrells Ford Primitive Camping Area 32
King Creek Falls 33
The Long Trails of the Headwaters 34
Reed Creek Bottoms 37

Chapter Three - The West Fork
West Fork Map 40
West Fork Overview 41
Floating the West Fork 41
The West Fork on Foot 43
Holcomb Creek Trail 43
Three Forks Trail 45
Overflow Road Primitive Camping Area 47

Chapter Four - Section II
Section II Map 50
Section II Overview 51
Floating Section II 51

Section II on Foot 55
Bartram & Chattooga River Trail 55
Willis Knob / Rocky Gap Horse Camp 57

Chapter Five - Section III
Section III Map 60
Section III Overview 61
Floating Section III 61
Section III on Foot 71
Earl's Ford 71
Sandy Ford 72
Dick's Creek Falls 74
US Hwy 76 bridge 75
Chattooga River Trail 76

Chapter Six - Section IV
Section IV Map 80
Section IV Overview 81
Floating Section IV 81
Section IV on Foot 92
Sutton's Hole 92
Woodall Shoals 93
Seven Foot Falls 94
Cliff Creek - Stekoa Creek 95
Long Creek Falls 97
Raven Cliffs 98
Opossum Creek Trail 100
Camp Creek 102

Chapter Seven - Rules & Regulations - Facts & Figures
Regulations of Use 106
Local Forest Service Information 106
Whitewater Ratings 107
Emergency Information 107
Floating Times 108
Chattooga Outfitters 109
Chattooga Usage Figures 110
Adopt-the-Chattooga 111
Comparative Trail Charts 112
Concerned Organizations 114
Area State Parks 115

Preface
Always Check the Weather Forecast

I still vividly recall the first time I laid eyes on *the* river. It was the late 1970's, and the Chattooga was one of the hottest attractions anywhere. I had heard firsthand the stories of its beautiful scenery, its blistering whitewater, and I had seen *the* movie which had made it famous. Now I wanted to see for myself what was so great about this mysterious place.

Having grown up in the Metro Atlanta area, family trips to the mountains were very common. Dahlonega, Cleveland, Vogel State Park, Blairsville, Franklin, Gatlinburg - these towns and their many interesting destinations were all old-hat, but for some reason I had never visited *the* river.

All of this changed as several college buddies got together and began to plan a hiking trip. We had heard about a trail outside of Clayton that followed the river, allowing hikers a good look at some of its alluring whitewater. We planned our route, studied the maps, and assembled all the needed equipment. We were sure it would be a good, if not uneventful trip.

Standing on the Hwy 76 bridge for the first time that sunny September day, the Chattooga immediately became a fixation. There was something captivating - something mysterious - about the way the river disappeared around the far bend, something powerful in the deliberate way the crystal water flowed over countless rocks in the river bed. To me, this was an unchartered wilderness, one begging to be experienced and explored. I couldn't wait for our hike to begin.

Our plan was rather simple: hike the Bartram Trail from Warwoman Dell east for about nine miles to the river. We would camp here, then turn south along the Chattooga River Trail for ten miles to Hwy 76. Simple. An easy two day hike.

Unfortunately, as is so often the case with great expectations, our trip did not turn out quite as expected. For starters, a general lack of knowledge on our part coupled with the absence of trail signs at a few key intersections resulted in our party reaching the river somewhere around Earl's Ford, several miles north of our intended destination. We knew *about* where we were, so we weren't worried. We were tired and a bit aggravated from the day's confusion, but enjoyed a well-deserved evening in camp. Unfortunately for us, the sunshine and warmth of early September departed that night, as a tropical storm came inland across the Florida panhandle.

By morning, this rude intruder had descended on our group by way of a cold, driving rain that made everything associated with camping and hiking miserable. Our carefully crafted plans to linger suddenly became obsolete, our prime directive being to get back to the car as quickly as possible.

It's at this point that the story becomes a bit fuzzy (selective amnesia). For some reason, in our haste, we left the trail, perhaps to shortcut one of the Chattooga River Trail's many broad loops. In any event, we literally spent hours stumbling along slippery river banks, wading through cold water, and climbing on all fours through some of the worst laurel thickets imaginable. To this day, I cannot recall why it took us so long to get back on the trail and reach 76, but we were all imagining sounds from the highway long before we reached it late that afternoon. I have never had worse blisters - ever.

One of my major goals for the hike went largely unaccomplished, as the path we took offered precious little exposure to the river. However, my first good look at Chattooga whitewater came that same day as we came along side *Bull Sluice* just as a group of about six kayakers ran the rain-swollen giant. Right then and there my affair with whitewater began - one that still continues.

I have twenty years worth of Chattooga memories now - dozens of pleasant trips along the river, both floating and hiking. A few bad ones stand out too, like some of my forced swims through *Bull Sluice* and the *Narrows*. (I guess I never really became a very good paddler.) But twenty years later, I can still stand on the 76 bridge and get excited about this place. Though I have hundreds of memories and dozens of stories, it is exciting to know that many more are yet to be written.

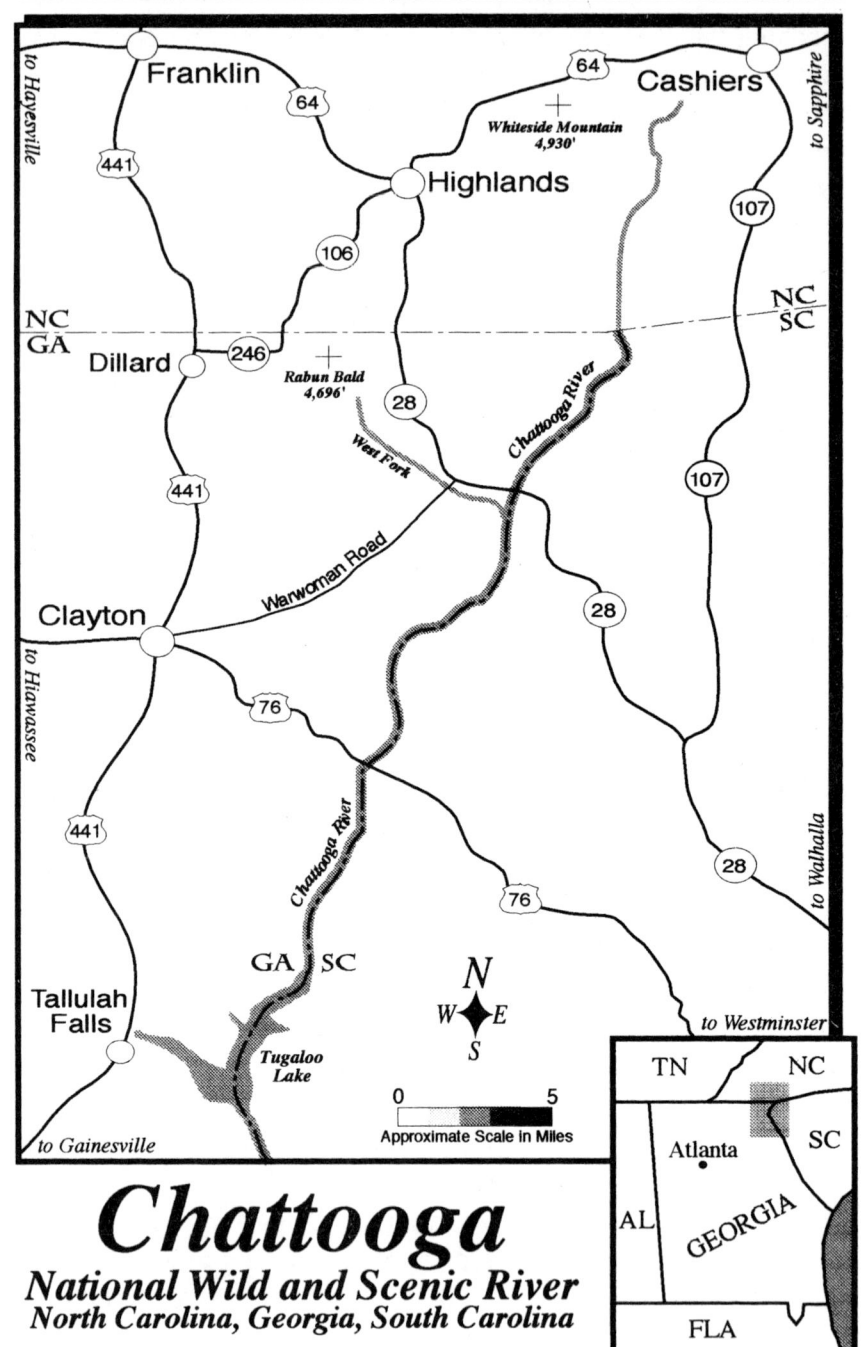

The CHATTOOGA
Wild and Scenic River

1

Introduction

Tiger Swallowtail butterflies gather on a sandbar along the upper Chattooga.

Introduction

The Chattooga River is truly one of the most beautiful and untamed rivers in our country today. Though its entire length is only fifty-seven miles, this river compensates with beauty and action what it may lack in overall size or length. From North Carolina's Whiteside Mountain to Lake Tugaloo on the Georgia - South Carolina border, the Chattooga is a study in motion, dropping over one-half mile in its short life. Falling at a pace exceeding the famed Colorado River, the Chattooga unleashes some of the Southeast's most formidable whitewater.

Wild and Scenic Designation

In 1968, the U.S. Congress passed the *National Wild and Scenic Rivers Act*, aimed at preserving many of our nation's premier waterways. Under this legislation, selected rivers are classified under the following categories:

1) **Wild** - unspoiled, undammed, with primitive surroundings, and accessible only by trail.
2) **Scenic** - undammed, with undeveloped shoreline, and accessible by road.
3) **Recreational** - easily accessible by road, with some development and preexisting dams allowed.

On May 10, 1974, the Chattooga was designated a member of the *National Wild and Scenic River* system by Congress. Of the Chattooga's 57 miles, 40 are classified as *wild*, two miles as *scenic*, and 15 miles as *recreational*. To ensure that the river stays as undisturbed as possible, and to offer visitors the highest quality experience, the Chattooga is enclosed within a protective 15,000 acre corridor that extends approximately one-quarter mile from the river banks. Except for road crossings, motorized vehicles are not allowed within the corridor (with one unfortunate exception - see Sandy Ford), and a strict set of usage guidelines govern boating, hiking and camping.

The Deliverance Factor

The Chattooga flowed relatively unknown to outsiders until the now infamous *Deliverance* was filmed here in 1972. Hollywood notables Burt Reynolds, Jon Voight, Ned Beatty and Ronny Cox starred in the production, whose river scenes were filmed on the Chattooga, in Tallulah Gorge, and on the nearby Chauga River in South Carolina. With the critical acclaim of the movie, thousands of ill-prepared boaters flocked to run the *"Deliverance River,"* resulting in some very grim statistics.

From 1970 to 1975, eighteen people lost their lives on the Chattooga, most as a result of not wearing a personal floatation device (PFD). Early stories about river usage contain references to people running Class IV-V whitewater with inner tubes, cheap rafts and even homemade crafts that defy description. PFDs were usually an afterthought, and good times on the river often involved alcohol - a real recipe for disaster.

After its inclusion into the *National Wild and Scenic River* system, the Forest Service introduced strict boating regulations designed to improve safety. Fatalities on the river were drastically reduced, though over thirty have now died since the early 1970's.

Crowds flock to the river in greater numbers than ever - some to tackle the challenging whitewater - others to fish, hike, or just take in the outstanding scenery. Truly the river has something to offer everyone. But today's Chattooga is just as threatened as ever. Pressure from encroaching development, increased use, logging, erosion, pollution and other factors require that stewards of this magnificent resource stay ever vigilant. As visitors in this wild area, each of us must look for ways to help in the fight to keep the Chattooga River forever wild and free.

Origins

"Chattooga" or "Chatuga"

"*Chattooga*" or "*Chatuga*" has been translated *"we crossed here"*, and appears several times in Cherokee culture. Other possible derivations may have their origins in words meaning *"I have crossed,"* or even *"he drank by sips,"* among others. The word may originally be of Creek Indian origin, as the Creeks once occupied this region before the Cherokee.

Geography & Topography

The Chattooga River is born high on the Blue Ridge Escarpment region of the Southern Appalachian mountains. Here the rolling terrain of the Carolina piedmont rises several thousand feet in dramatic form as the Blue Ridge mountains. A number of sizable rivers flow from this steep escarpment along the eastern flank of the eastern continental divide. Among these are the Chattooga, Whitewater, Thompson, Horsepasture, Toxaway and Estatoe Rivers. These rivers all flow through deep, rugged gorges as they drop several thousand feet from the escarpment to the piedmont region of South Carolina.

While by whitewater standards the Chattooga is an extremely steep river, by comparison with its escarpment neighbors, it is actually quite mild. From Cashiers, N.C. to Lake Tugaloo, the Chattooga drops almost 2,500', for an average of just over 49 feet per mile. In comparison, rivers such as the Whitewater, Horsepasture and Toxaway can average several hundred feet per mile!

The primary reason for this difference is that the Chattooga flows roughly parallel to the escarpment and to the west of a spur ridge which separates it from the piedmont, while the other rivers flow directly across the escarpment. In other words, the Chattooga roughly follows the escarpment backbone, while the others fall directly off the side. For this reason the Chattooga is a much longer river.

Chattooga Flora

The forests of the Southern Appalachians are known to contain more than one-half of the known species of trees, ferns and flowering plants in North America. Over 130 different species of trees alone have been identified in this region - more than anywhere else on the North American continent. Primarily due to the diversity of topography and the dramatic change in elevation from Cashiers to Lake Tugaloo, the Chattooga contains a wide variety of forest types. Due to the tremendous diversity of growth conditions, a wide variety of plant and animal species can be found within a relatively small geographic area.

Chattooga corridor communities

Six different natural environments have been identified in the river corridor. They are the *river banks and alder zones, floodplain forests, cove and slope forests, ridge tops and upland oak forests, pitch pine-oak communities* and *cliff / gorge wall communities.*

River bank zone. Soils in this area are usually rocky or sandy. The most common trees here are the sycamore, sweetgum and persimmon. Shrubs present may include viburnum, mountain laurel, and rhododendron.

Floodplain forests. These are normally found between the river bank zone and the slope forests, and have usually been altered to some degree by humans due to their attractiveness to agricultural activities in the past. The most common hardwoods here are sweetgum, red maple, tulip-poplar, dogwood, sourwood and sassafras. Conifers found here include the shortleaf pine, white pine and Virginia pine. At higher elevations hemlock becomes more common. Shrubs present may include wild hydrangea, spicebush and strawberry bush.

Cove forests. Somewhat rare due to the relative absence of streams which flow north, the Chattooga possesses only a handful of these environments, most notably southwest of Ellicott Rock in Georgia and within the Rock Gorge. The most common trees found here include tulip-poplar, hemlock, basswood, red oak, dogwood, red maple and pawpaw. Shrubs found here include rosebay rhododendron, sweetshrub, leucothoe (dog hobble) and holly.

Slope forests. These occur up slope from the damper cove forests, and can often contain species more common to the ridge top forests. Common hardwoods found here include hickories, tulip-poplar, black oak, northern oak, white oak, black gum, red maple, beech, sourwood, dogwood and black locust. Prevalent shrubs include rosebay rhododendron, carolina laurel and mountain laurel.

Ridge Tops and Upland Oak Forests. The relatively drier conditions in these areas support several species of oaks, including scarlet oak, white oak, and chestnut oak. Other species present include mockernut hickory, sourwood, dogwood, black locust, persimmon and blackgum. Shrubs present include mountain laurel, leadplant, buffalo nut and fringe tree.

Pitch-pine communities. These dry southern-exposed communities are usually found on a ridge top or high slope separating coves. Species present include southern red oak, blackjack oak, post oak, pitch pine, scarlet oak, blackgum and sourwood. Prevalent shrubs include horse-sugar, sweetfern, bristly locust and blueberry.

Cliffs and Gorge Walls. Cliffs and large areas of exposed rocks occur at numerous points along the river, particularly at the Chattooga Cliffs and several points below Woodall Shoals. These rock communities are generally classified as either wetter or drier, depending upon the amount of seepage or spray which contacts the area. The wetter communities generally feature hemlock and sphagnum moss, while the drier usually features white pine and rock spikemoss.

Wildflowers and Flowering Plants

The Southern Appalachians contain an abundance of beautiful flowering plants. The tremendous diversity of forest types, coupled with generous amounts of moisture, create an environment in which a multitude of these beautiful species may flourish. Be sure to carry a wildflower guide when hiking to aid in identification of these fascinating plants. Below is a list of some of these plants and the season they normally bloom.

sessile trillium	early spring
Oconee Bells	early spring
great white trillium	spring
painted trillium	spring
Solomon's seal	spring
sweet white violet	spring
bird foot violet	spring
common blue violet	spring
dog hobble	mid-spring
wood anemone	spring
Vassey's trillium	spring
rue anemone	spring
trout lily	spring
Hepatica	spring
mayapple	spring
bellwort	spring
wild geranium	spring
bloodroot	spring
jack-in-the-pulpit	spring
dwarf crest iris	spring
flame azalea	late spring
mountain laurel	late spring
galax	late spring
rosebay rhododendron	early summer
Indian pipe	summer
spotted wintergreen	summer
rattlesnake plaintain	summer
Michaux's lily	late summer

Chattooga Fauna

The same conditions which contribute to the tremendous diversity of plants also helps maintain a wide range of animal life in the river corridor. The following are lists of animals that are present in certain ecosystems along the river.

Birds of the Chattooga Corridor

While many species of birds make the Chattooga region their home year-round, other species are seasonal or appear in the region during periods of migration. Consult your field guide for specific information. The following are a portion of the species which have been observed in the Chattooga region:

Black-throated Blue Warbler	Hooded Warbler
Black-and-White Warbler	Pine Warbler
Canada Warbler	Scarlet Tanager
Common Raven	Red-eyed Vireo
Solitary Vireo	Yellow-Throated Vireo
Gray Catbird	Blue Jay
Carolina Chickadee	Tufted Titmouse
Coopers Hawk	Broad-winged Hawk
Red-tailed Hawk	Ruffed Grouse
Wild Turkey	Eastern Screech Owl
Great Horned Owl	Barred Owl
Whip-poor-will	Pileated Woodpecker
Downy Woodpecker	Red-cockaded Woodpeckers
White-breasted Nuthatch	Red-breasted Nuthatch
Brown-headed Nuthatch	Golden-crowned Kinglets
American Robin	Carolina Wren
Winter Wren	Woodthrush
Northern Cardinal	Dark-eyed Junco
Great Blue Heron	Green-backed Heron
Belted Kingfisher	Spotted Sandpiper
Wood Ducks	Mallard Ducks
Southern Bald Eagle	Golden Eagle
Osprey	Peregrine Falcon
Canada Geese	Ruby-throated Hummingbird

Mammals of the Chattooga Corridor

Black bear	Big brown bat	Southeastern shrew
Beaver	Red bat	Least shrew
Muskrat	Little brown bat	Smoky shrew
White-tailed deer	Northern red-eared bat	Eastern mole
Raccoon	Silver-haired bat	Deer mouse
Opossum	Eastern spotted skunk	White-footed mouse
Bobcat	Striped skunk	Golden mouse
Gray fox	Mink	Eastern wood rat
Eastern cottontail	Long-tailed weasel	Feral (wild) dogs
Eastern chipmunk	Gray squirrel	Feral (wild) hogs

Fish of the Chattooga River and its tributaries

For many, fishing is the ultimate Chattooga activity, particularly *trout* fishing. The Chattooga has a solid reputation as a trout stream, particularly the area above the Highwy 28 bridge and around Burrells Ford. Chattooga tributaries such as the East Fork and West Fork are also very popular.

Three species of trout occur in the Chattooga watershed. *Brook trout,* a native species, normally occur only in the upper tributary streams, and rarely exceed six to eight inches in length. *Rainbow and Brown trout*, both non-native species to the Southern Appalachians, occur in the main river, particularly above Highway 28. These species are also stocked by truck and by helicopter on a regular basis. Additionally, the following species may be present in the main river or tributaries:

Redeye bass	Redbreast sunfish
Largemouth bass	Green sunfish
Bluegill	Flat bullhead
Northern hogsucker	Striped jumprock
River chub	Hornyhead chub
Saffron shiner	Whitetail shiner
Yellowfin shiner	Turquoise darter

Reptiles and Amphibians

The Southern Appalacians feature an impressive array of reptiles and amphibians. Salamanders in particular thrive in the streams and moist coves of the region. The following is a sampling of the reptiles and amphibians one may encounter:

Spotted salamander	Marbled salamander
Tiger salamander	long-tailed salamander
Brook salamander	Red salamander
Four-toed salamander	Eastern newt
American toad	Southern toad
Chorus frog	Spring peeper
Green frog	Bullfrog
Southern leopard frog	Snapping turtle
Musk turtle	Eastern box turtle
Slider	Softshell turtle
Ground skink	Five-lined skink
Racer	Ringneck snake
Rat snake	Eastern hognose snake
Kingsnake	Northern water snake
Eastern ribbon snake	Garter snake
Copperhead*	Timber rattlesnake*

A note about snakes: Many hikers seem to live in mortal fear of encountering a poisonous snake while out on the trail. While an abundance of these reptiles thrive in the Chattooga watershed, your chances of encountering a poisonous variety are actually very slim.

The species most often mistaken for poisonous is the Northern water snake, which reaches lengths of 2' - 4'. These snakes have crossbands on the neck and back with a stout body. They frequent just about any type of freshwater and become quite aggressive when threatened. Northern water snakes are frequently mistaken for the copperhead, which is usually orange or pinkish with bold red-brown crossbands. Unless you are familiar with snakes, the best advice is to give them all a wide berth.

Weather and Climate

The Chattooga flows through one of the rainiest regions in the continental United States. Warm, moisture laden air blowing inland from the Gulf of Mexico and the Atlantic Ocean slam headlong into the Southeastern Blue Ridge Escarpment as it rises dramatically from the flat piedmont region. This results in rainfall nearly double what some locations in the nearby flat lands might receive in any given year.

Overall, the river climate can be divided into two distinct zones. The northern half of the corridor has colder winters and milder summers, and is generally much wetter. Rainfall can average up to an astonishing 80" per year. The southern half of the river averages 50" - 60" of rainfall per year. Here the winters are generally cool and the summers relatively hot.

Snowfall occurs several times per year in the lower corridor, averaging only a few inches per year, while the northernmost peaks near Cashiers can receive several feet per year. The average annual snowfall for the entire river corridor is only 3" - 4" per year.

Rainfall can occur any time of the year, but the wettest months are generally January, February, March and July, and the driest months are May, September and October. A dramatic variety of weather conditions can occur throughout the year.

Approximate Average Temperatures

Lower Corridor

Month	High	Low
Jan	42	20
Feb	45	22
Mar	50	25
Apr	70	43
May	77	46
Jun	87	59
Jul	92	62
Aug	88	60
Sep	82	57
Oct	71	42
Nov	63	36
Dec	52	28

Ellicott Rock

Month	High	Low
Jan	32	10
Feb	36	14
Mar	42	16
Apr	61	34
May	68	37
Jun	78	50
Jul	83	53
Aug	80	52
Sep	73	50
Oct	62	33
Nov	54	28
Dec	43	20

River Safety

Hand-in-hand with the Chattooga's notoriety for thrilling whitewater is the reputation it has earned over the years as a *very* dangerous river. According to U.S. Forest Service statistics kept since 1970, *thirty-five fatalities* and numerous other near-fatalities have occurred on the river. Eighteen of these deaths occurred from 1970 - 1975, most of these before strict boater regulations took effect in 1975.

Anyone thinking about taking a trip down the Chattooga should consider obtaining a copy of this fatality report, as it very ably demonstrates the case for proper equipment, training, expertise and caution. *A number of experienced boaters have been killed running the Chattooga.*

In the early days of the Chattooga's popularity, many of the deaths which occurred on the river resulted from boaters without PFDs overturning in fast water. Some unfortunate victims, while wearing PFDs, had them torn off in the violent currents which exist around some of the larger rapids. There have been several fatalities involving persons swimming in the river, with at least two of these occurring at *Bull Sluice*.

The Most Dangerous Spots on the Chattooga

Forest Service statistics indicate at least three locations on the river which demand the utmost respect of both boaters and those on foot - *Bull Sluice* (9 deaths), *Woodall Shoals* (7 deaths) and the *Five Falls* area (11 deaths). While these numbers are dramatic, consideration must be made for the huge numbers of people visiting the river each year, particularly boaters (see chapter seven). While total boating use has gone from approximately 800 in 1970 to nearly 90,000 in 1995, fatalities on the river have averaged less than one per year since 1975.

Considering the sheer volume of paddlers and the level of the river when some of these trips are attempted, it is perhaps surprising that even with the registration and regulation of paddlers the number of fatalities is not higher. *It is also worth noting that there has never been a fatality on the river involving a commercial trip.*

Chattooga Fatalities 1970 - January 1998

Year	Fatality	Type	Location	Explanation
1970	1	no info.	Woodall Shoals	no information provided
1971	2	no info.	Bull Sluice	no information provided
1972	1	boating	Woodall Shoals	no PFD
1972	1	boating	Narrows	no information provided
1972	1	boating	Bull Sluice	no PFD
1972	1	boating	Bull Sluice	no PFD
1973	1	boating	Woodall Shoals	injuries/exposure
1973	1	boating	Bull Sluice	no PFD
1973	1	boating	Narrows	no PFD
1973	1	boating	Woodall Shoals	no PFD
1973	1	tubing	Bull Sluice	no PFD
1974	1	boating	Woodall Shoals	no PFD
1974	1	boating	Crack-in-the-Rock	foot entrapment
1974	1	swimming	Earl's Ford	caught in current
1975	1	boating	Fall Creek area	hypothermia
1975	1	swimming	Thrift's Ferry	calm water drowning
1975	1	boating	Soc-em-dog	pinned in river
1979	1	hiking	Woodall Shoals	fell into river
1979	1	boating	Jawbone	pinned in river
1980	1	boating	Crack-in-the-Rock	pinned in river
1981	1	boating	Bull Sluice	foot entrapment
1981	1	swimming	Bull Sluice	foot entrapment
1984	1	hiking	Woodall Shoals	tree fell, pinned in river
1989	1	boating	Crack-in-the-Rock	pinned in river
1990	1	boating	Narrows	foot entrapment
1991	1	boating	Five Falls	caught in current/injuries
1992	1	tubing	Five Falls	no PFD
1993	1	boating	Five Falls	flipped/caught in current
1994	1	boating	Dick's Cr. Ledge	river at flood stage
1995	1	boating	Five Falls	pinned in river
1996	1	boating	Crack-in-the-Rock	pinned in river
1997	1	swimming	Bull Sluice	victim could not swim
1997	1	boating	below 7 Foot Falls	heart attack
1998	1	boating	Soc-em-dog	pinned in river

This information is further detailed in a report available from the U.S. Forest Service office in Walhalla, S.C. The report also lists near-fatal accidents which have occurred on the river since 1970. This information is provided in the hopes that those planning to visit the Chattooga will realize the very real dangers present here, regardless of the activity.

Chattooga Region History

Cherokee Empire

Native Americans ruled North America long before the first Europeans landed in what would eventually become the United States. A band of Native Americans known as the Cherokee ruled the Southern Appalachians, controlling a region perhaps as vast as 40,000 square miles, extending from Virginia to Alabama. Though no definite date can be determined, some historians believe the Cherokee have inhabited the Southern Appalachians for as much as 1,000 years before the first white explorers arrived.

At the time of first contact, the Cherokees had large settlements along the headwaters of the major river systems of the southeast, including the Chattooga. As the Europeans moved further into the wilderness, the Cherokee were forced to establish new settlements in more remote locations.

From the time of first contact until their forced removal in 1838, Cherokee contact with European settlers increased. Much of this contact revolved around trading, particularly in pelts. In the early 1700's this industry had progressed to the point that the colony of South Carolina was regulating it. Trading was made easier due to the presence of an extensive series of trails, the most prominent of which was the *Cherokee Path*.

One of these paths went through *Chattooga Town*, a Cherokee settlement of nearly 100 individuals located along the Chattooga in the broad floodplain in the Long Bottom Ford area. Though small in comparison to most settlements, the area most likely held some importance due to its location along a major path. In any event, it seems that by the mid-1700's the settlement had all but disappeared, though individual families may have remained until the early 1800's.

The bitter removal of the Cherokee from the region was enacted in 1838 - the infamous "Trail of Tears". Approximately 4,000 Cherokee died of exposure and disease as they were impounded and suffered a forced march to Oklahoma. A small group of Cherokee escaped and hid out in the mountains. This group eventually became known as the Eastern Band of the Cherokee, whose descendants now reside in Cherokee, N.C.

European Exploration and Settlement

The Spanish explorer Hernando De Soto is believed to have marched through the area with a small army in 1540. Primarily driven by a search for gold, De Soto may have crossed the Chattooga River somewhere in the vicinity of Burrells Ford, although there is a good deal of disagreement on this.

In the late 1600's English explorers and settlers were venturing deeper into the wilderness of the Southern Appalachians, primarily as a transportation corridor to the French-controlled areas west of the mountains along the Tennessee River. Indian traders and professional hunters were the leaders in opening this rugged region.

By 1760, the relationship between the English and the Cherokee had deteriorated, and the war which followed resulted in a loss of much Cherokee territory. By the time American colonists declared their independence in 1776, the English and Cherokee had completed their skirmish, and were now united to fight against the Americans. This war resulted in the Cherokee being pushed even deeper into the remote mountain region.

Tensions with the Cherokee continued to remain high through the 1780's, resulting in the construction of several military outposts along the South Carolina frontier. One of these, Oconee Station, was constructed in Oconee County, S.C. in the early 1790's. (It is currently a South Carolina park, and is open to the public.) After tensions with the Cherokee had settled down by 1793, the facility served as a trading post.

William Bartram and Andre Michaux

Among the most famous early explorers to this region were the American botanist, artist and writer William Bartram and the French botanist Andre Michaux. Bartram traversed the area extensively from 1773 to 1778, and published a book on the subject in 1791. The famous Bartram Trail which traverses portions of the Chattooga corridor honor Bartram's travels.

Andre Michaux explored the Southern Appalachian region in a quest for botanical specimens for the French Royal Court, and is reported to have crossed the Chattooga in 1787. After a difficult and disappointing expedition, Michaux abandoned his trek, only to later discover the rare and elusive *Oconee Bells* wildflower.

The Blue Ridge (Black Diamond) Railroad

This failed project, chartered in 1852, was to have linked Charleston, S.C. with Cincinnati, OH. by way of railroad. The proposed line was to run through Anderson and Walhalla, up and over the Chattooga Ridge, descend into Rabun Gap, then turn down the Little Tennessee River and proceed to Knoxville. One of the line's biggest projects was the Stumphouse Tunnel near Walhalla. Over 4,000 feet of the proposed tunnel had been completed by the time work was stopped in 1859. The project was halted for good with the outbreak of Civil War hostilities in 1861. Had the railroad been completed, it may have rewritten the history of the region dramatically. Visitors to the Stumphouse Tunnel Park near Walhalla can still gaze into the old, abandoned tunnel.

Twentieth Century Milestones

From the early 1900's up to around 1920, timber interests began purchasing and logging in the Southern Appalachians, including the Chattooga watershed. Technological improvements made it possible for entire forests to be cut over with little if any attention given to reforestation. The resulting damage effects forest soils to this day. After authorization in 1911, the Forest Service began buying land for watershed protection and reforestation.

During the Great Depression of the 1930's, the Civilian Conservation Corps (CCC) completed many lasting projects in the Chattooga area. Among these were the Stumphouse Ranger Station, the Chattooga and Yellow Branch picnic areas, Oconee State Park, the Walhalla Fish Hatchery and the modernization of many of the area's roads.

The CHATTOOGA
Wild and Scenic River

2

The Chattooga Headwaters

Stairstepping shoals along the Chattooga River near the entrance to the rugged Rock Gorge.

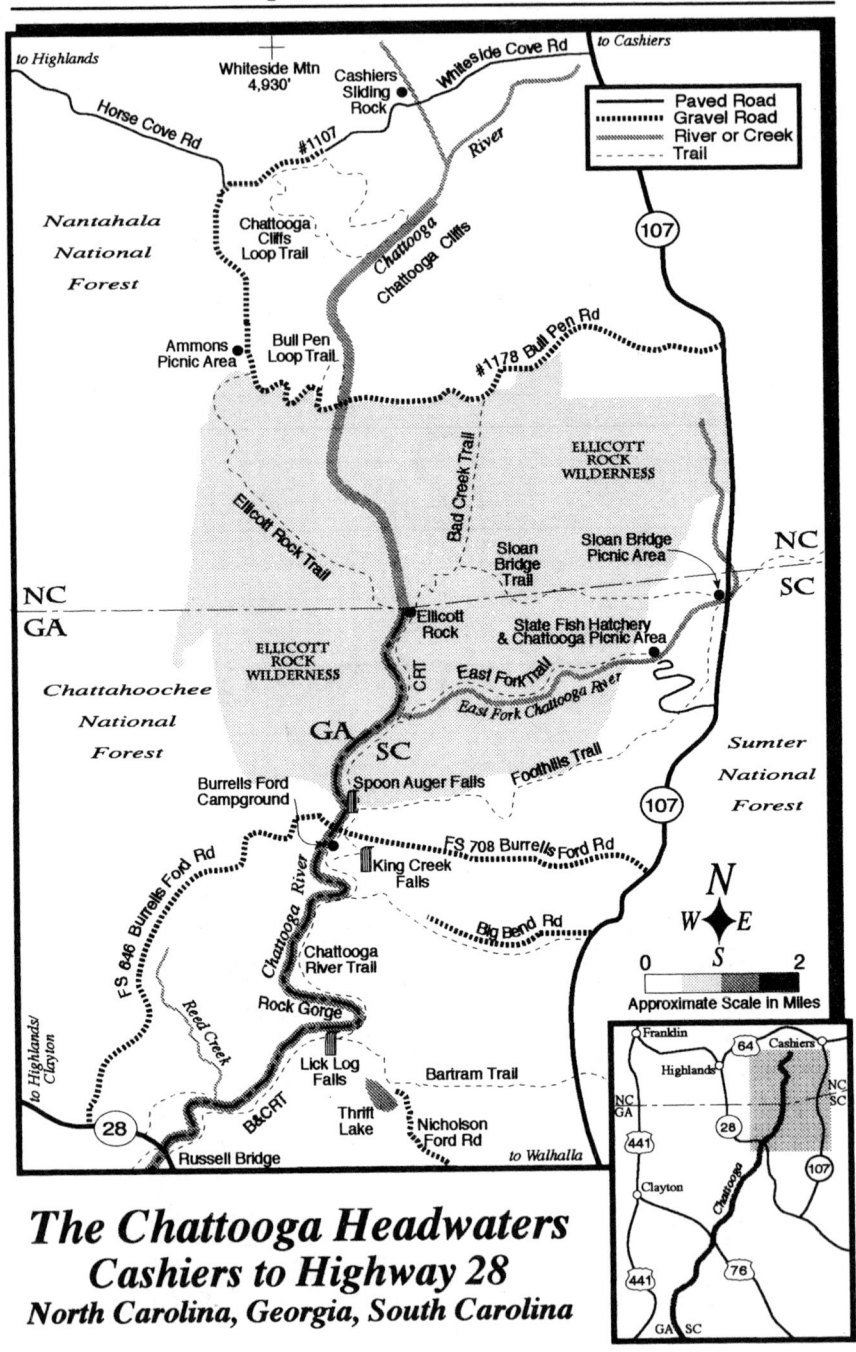

The Chattooga Headwaters
Cashiers to Highway 28
North Carolina, Georgia, South Carolina

The Headwaters

Whiteside Mountain to Highway 28

Pristine wilderness and magnificent scenery.

The Chattooga Wild and Scenic River is born high on the rocky cliffs of ancient Whiteside Mountain just west of Cashiers, NC. Beginning rather unspectacularly as a tiny rivulet, the Chattooga flows south off a rugged escarpment. Within its first ten miles, scores of tiny tributaries pour in, swelling the volume of the river considerably. By the time the Chattooga passes Ellicott Rock at the Georgia, North Carolina and South Carolina lines, it has grown into a very respectable mountain stream averaging 60 feet or more in width.

Below Ellicott Rock the river becomes the boundary between Georgia and South Carolina, flowing ten highly scenic miles down to Russell bridge at Highway 28. Below Highway 28 the river is open to boaters, but the northernmost twenty miles must be met on foot. This spectacular region is remote, dense forest and often hazardous to explore. From its origins, the river plunges nearly 2,000 feet on its journey to Russell bridge, creating a steep, scenic watershed that begs to be explored. If your only exposure to the Chattooga has been via its pounding whitewater, you may be in for a real treat as you discover the Chattooga's hidden treasure - the Headwaters region.

Whiteside Mountain Trail
Nantahala National Forest, Jackson County, NC

Trail length: 2 mile loop trail
Difficulty: Moderate
Elevation change: Approx. 500 feet
Features: National Recreational Trail, sheer cliffs, views
USGS Quadrangle Map: Highlands

Directions: Whiteside Mountain is located five miles east of Highlands and 5 miles west of Cashiers, NC just off Hwy 64. The turnoff is at the Jackson / Macon county line at the famous "Big View" overlook. Turn south onto Whiteside Mountain Road (#1690) and proceed approximately one mile to the large parking area on the left.

Though some might consider it unusual to list a mountain trail in a guide on the Chattooga River, there is no better place to get an overall view of the Chattooga watershed than from the summit of Whiteside Mountain. At 4,930 feet, Whiteside Mountain is one of the tallest peaks in the region, and is considered by geologists to be one of the oldest mountains in the world. Strikingly unique when viewed from the south, Whiteside features the highest sheer cliffs in the U.S. - over 750 feet. Overall, the mountain (known as *"the sitting down place"* to Native Americans) rises 2,000 feet above the south valley floor, providing stunning views of the surrounding Blue Ridge.

The moderate two mile loop trail begins at the parking area, and follows a rocky road bed for three-quarters of a mile up the northeast side of the mountain to a clearing. The trail then turns sharply right and begins to follow the high ridge line for 0.7 mile along the edge of the mountain's famous cliffs up to its rocky summit. With a good map one can plot the Chattooga's course southwest for nearly its entire length. Beyond the summit, the trail skirts Wildcat Cliffs before beginning a steep descent back to the parking area along a steep series of switchbacks. (Brochures are available at the parking area.)

Cashiers Sliding Rock
Nantahala National Forest, Jackson County, NC

Trail length: Several hundred yards
Difficulty: Moderate
Elevation change: Minimal
Features: Sliding rock on Chattooga River
USGS Quadrangle Map: Cashiers

Directions: *From the intersection of US Hwy 64 and Hwy 107 in Cashiers, proceed south on Hwy 107 for 1.7 miles. Turn right onto Whiteside Cove Road (#1107) and follow for 2.6 miles to the bridge or proceed several hundred yards further to a small parking area on the right.*

A small pocket of National Forest land completely surrounded by private property offers visitors a chance to explore a scenic stretch of the upper Chattooga near Cashiers. This portion of river features a smooth ten foot ledge known locally as *"Cashiers Sliding Rock"*. A thin padding of water provides the perfect medium for a plunge over the ledge into a frigid pool. Use a bit of discretion here, as numerous potholes and rough spots make this ride far from a sure thing.

During the summer months quite a crowd can assemble to enjoy the water slide and wade in the broad pool below. The river upstream of *Sliding Rock* is also quite scenic, featuring numerous splashing shoals. For spectacular views of Whiteside Mountain's famous cliffs, continue on Whiteside Cove Road.

Cashiers Sliding Rock

Chattooga Cliffs Trail
Nantahala National Forest, Macon County, NC

Trail length: 2.9 mile loop trail
Difficulty: Moderate
Elevation change: Approx. 450 feet
Features: Scenic views of Chattooga Cliffs
USGS Quadrangle Map: Highlands

Directions: *From Cashiers, follow the directions to Sliding Rock, then proceed along Whiteside Cove Road for an additional 4.5 miles (7.1 miles from Hwy 107) to FS 2052 on the left. From Highlands, proceed south on Main Street, which turns into Horse Cove Road. Follow for 4.5 miles to the intersection with Bull Pen Road and Whiteside Cove Road. Bear left onto Whiteside Cove Road and proceed 0.4 mile to FS 2052. Park here (do not block the gate).*

The *Chattooga Cliffs Trail* is a fairly new addition to the Chattooga's system of trails, and features nice views of the scenic *Chattooga Cliffs*. The trail initially follows FS 2052 above splashing Cane Creek. At approximately 1.0 mile look for a side trail to the left and follow this path on a moderate 0.2 mile descent along scenic Holly Branch.

A rock-hopping crossing of Cane Creek must be made just before its junction with the *Chattooga River Trail* (currently not connected to the trail of the same name below Ellicott Rock) which runs upstream along the river from Bull Pen bridge. Turn left onto this path and follow upstream along the river, keeping a sharp eye out for views of the Chattooga Cliffs to the east. Turn left onto an old logging road after 0.3 mile and begin a long, uphill one mile climb back out to Whiteside Cove Road on the Macon / Jackson County line. Turn left and walk approximately 0.4 mile back to your vehicle to complete the loop.

Bull Pen Bridge (Iron Bridge) Trail
Nantahala National Forest, Macon County, NC

Trail length: 1.0 mile loop
Difficulty: Moderate
Elevation change: Approx. 200 feet
Features: Outstanding gorge scenery
USGS Quadrangle Map: Highlands

Directions: *From Highlands, proceed south on Main Street, which turns into Horse Cove Road. Follow for 4.5 miles and turn right onto Bull Pen Road. Drive 3 miles to the iron bridge spanning the river. From Cashiers, drive south on Hwy 107 for approximately 6 miles and turn right onto Bull Pen Road (#1178). Proceed 5 miles to the bridge.*

One of the most scenic areas of the Chattooga River is the area surrounding the old iron *"government bridge"* on Bull Pen Road. Here the river plunges through a rugged gorge, squeezed between huge boulders and giant rock slabs before plunging over an impressive ledge directly beneath the bridge.

Iron Bridge on Bull Pen Road

A delightful one mile loop trail leads upstream from the bridge, passing more impressive scenery than can be described here. The first few hundred yards are particularly rugged, with steep side paths dropping down to some of the more scenic areas. Use caution here, as the river banks and rocks are very slippery! Several hundred yards above the bridge, the Chattooga calms and the trail drops alongside the river, providing access to several small sandy beaches and numerous emerald green pools.

Approximately one-half mile upstream from the bridge, the trail turns back sharply to the left and climbs several hundred feet to an old logging road as it begins to wind south. The trail passes an upper parking area off Bull Pen Road before turning sharply east and dropping back to the original trail head at the bridge.

Trail Note: *Due to extensive flood and snow damage over the past five years, the Forest Service recommends that hikers not attempt the riverside trail which stretches over three miles from Bull Pen bridge up to Whiteside Cove Road. Missing bridges and additional obstacles could create hazards. Further complicating this issue is a private property concern at the northern trail head. Check with the Forest Service office near Highlands for updates on this trail.*

Ellicott Rock Wilderness
North Carolina, South Carolina, Georgia

Directions: *The Ellicott Rock Wilderness is located approximately ten miles south of Cashiers, NC, and is roughly centered around the junction of North Carolina, South Carolina and Georgia. It can be accessed from Bull Pen Road, Burrells Ford Road or Hwy 107. See trail listings for specific directions.*

Ellicott Rock Wilderness is a beautiful 9,012 acre natural oasis which was designated as a unit of the National Wilderness System in 1975. Since its inception this protected wilderness has grown from 3,300 acres to 9,012 acres, and the Forest Service has recommended a 2,000 acre addition to the wilderness in the Sumter National Forest. Elevations range from around 2,100' along the lower Chattooga to 3,294' atop South Carolina's second highest peak, Fork Mountain.

Because of its Wilderness designation, this area is closed to horses, bicycles and motorized vehicles of any type. Primitive camping is allowed, but the Forest Service has specific guidelines that campers must abide by.

The wilderness area is named for Major Andrew Ellicott, a Lancaster, PA. surveyor hired to determine the correct boundary line between Georgia and North Carolina. Previously Ellicott had been a member of survey teams working on high profile projects such as extending the *Mason-Dixon* line and surveying the site of Washington D.C. in the early 1790's.

The need for Ellicott's services was due to a 1803 claim made by the State of Georgia to a large piece of property in what was considered to be North Carolina. The real problem was that the two states could not agree where the 35th parallel, the boundary line, was really located. In 1804 Georgia's "occupation" of what came to be known as the *Orphan Strip* erupted into violence as imprisonments, riots, assaults and woundings became common on both sides. Governors from the two states finally appointed commissioners to establish the correct border.

In 1807 commissioners from both states discovered that the boundary line claimed by Georgia was in error by upwards of 22 miles, but still could not determine the exact boundary. In 1809, David B. Mitchell was elected governor of Georgia, and immediately began efforts to determine the exact location of the 35th parallel.

Ellicott and his team completed their surveying work late in 1811. The only lasting visible evidence was a rock along the river marked *"N"* on the north side *"G"* on the south. Another team working on the North Carolina / South Carolina border came through the area in 1813, and created the well-known inscription *"LAT 35 AD 1813 NC + SC"* which is now known as *"Commissioners Rock"*. The real Ellicott Rock is said to be located anywhere from a few yards to several hundred feet from Commissioners Rock.

Subsequent surveys have shown Ellicott's work to be surprisingly accurate considering the equipment available in 1811. The boundary question continued to surface into the twentieth century, as one report stated that Georgia Governor Jimmy Carter had a commission investigate the boundary issue in the early 1970's.

A much more detailed examination of this fascinating subject was written by Harry R. Wright and published in the March and April, 1971 issues of *GA. Magazine*. Even more details can be found in *Andrew Ellicott - His Life and Letters*.

Commissioner's Rock

Bad Creek Trail
Ellicott Rock Wilderness, Nantahala Natl. Forest, Jackson County, NC

Trail length: 3.5 miles one way
Difficulty: Moderate
Elevation change: Approx. 800 feet
Features: Ellicott Rock, Commissioner's Rock
USGS Quadrangle Map: Cashiers

Directions: *From Cashiers, proceed south on Hwy 107 for approximately seven miles to Bull Pen Road (#1178) on the right. Follow Bull Pen Road west for three miles to the wilderness marker and trail head on the left. Park well off the road.*

The Bad Creek Trail is a moderate 3.5 mile path that meanders along a forested ridge top before plunging into the Chattooga gorge and intersecting the Chattooga River Trail just north of famed Ellicott Rock. This orange-blazed path initially follows an old jeep road, crossing the wilderness boundary approximately two miles from the trail head. Just beyond, the path intersects the Sloan Bridge Trail from the east. From here, a long series of switchbacks descend to the river.

Once alongside the Chattooga, the path proceeds south for several hundred yards to the trail sign announcing your arrival at Ellicott Rock. A short, steep descent along the overgrown river bank will bring you to the 1813 *"Commissioner's Rock"* marker. Though over 185 years old, the famous chiseled signpost remains.

Ellicott Rock Trail
Ellicott Rock Wilderness, Nantahala Natl. Forest, Macon County, NC

Trail length: 3.5 miles one way
Difficulty: Moderate
Elevation change: Approx. 700 feet
Features: Ellicott Rock / Commissioner's Rock
USGS Quadrangle Map: Highlands & Cashiers

Directions: *From Cashiers, follow directions to Bad Creek Trail and continue three miles to the trail head. From Highlands, drive south on Main Street, which becomes Horse Cove Road, for 4.5 miles and turn right onto Bull Pen Road. Proceed 1.8 miles to the trail head on the right.*

For hikers who desire a bit more adventure, this path to Ellicott Rock may be just what you're looking for. Though trail length and elevation change are almost identical, the Ellicott Rock Trail route requires a Chattooga River crossing which could prove to be a wet experience.

From the trail head, this path follows an old logging road for nearly two undulating miles. As the trail nears the river, it steepens and reaches a fork. To the left a narrow path descends along a series of switchbacks, while to the right a larger path continues straight ahead down a gentler grade (crossing into Georgia) before terminating at a primitive camping area along the river.

Regardless of the route, hikers must wade across the Chattooga to reach Chattooga River Trail and Ellicott Rock. At normal to low water levels, this crossing should be no more than knee-deep on a average adult, though the current is surprisingly strong in some spots. *Use extreme caution anytime you try to cross a stream. Foot entrapment in strong currents has killed a number of visitors to the Chattooga. Do not attempt to cross the river if the weather has been rainy for a prolonged period, or if the water is cloudy! If these conditions persist, access Ellicott Rock via the Bad Creek Trail.*

Sloan Bridge Trail
Ellicott Rock Wilderness, Nantahala Natl. Forest, Jackson County, NC

Trail length: 6.3 miles to junction; 7.5 miles to Ellicott Rock
Difficulty: Moderate
Elevation change: Approx. 800 feet
Features: Ellicott Rock / Commissioner's Rock
USGS Quadrangle Map: Cashiers

Directions: *From Cashiers, follow Hwy 107 approximately ten miles south to the Sloan Bridge Picnic Area. Sloan Bridge Picnic Area is located approximately one mile south of the North Carolina / South Carolina state line.*

Yet another route into this scenic area is the popular Sloan Bridge Trail. This path originates at the Sloan Bridge Picnic Area, which is also an access point for the famous Foothills Trail. From the picnic area, the Foothills Trail winds northeast for 4.4 miles to Whitewater Falls, and southwest for 3.3 miles to the fish hatchery road.

Leaving the trail head, the Sloan Bridge Trail heads west alternately ascending and descending as it works its way along the rugged northern slopes of 3,294' Fork Mountain. At mile point 6.3 the path reaches a junction with the Bad Creek Trail 1.2 miles from the river and just a few hundred yards upstream of Ellicott Rock.

The sheer number of good trails in this area makes it possible to engineer a wide variety of possible hikes, from short afternoon jaunts to multi-day backpacking trips. Be aware that the trails in this area can become somewhat crowded in the summer, especially on the weekends. By avoiding peak periods visitors may be able to maximize their wilderness experience.

East Fork Trail
Ellicott Rock Wilderness, Sumter Natl. Forest, Oconee County, SC

Trail length: 2.5 miles one way
Difficulty: Moderate
Elevation change: Approx. 400 feet
Features: Beautiful stream
USGS Quadrangle Map: Tamassee

Directions: *From Cashiers, follow Hwy 107 south for 11.7 miles (3.5 miles south of the state line) and turn right at the sign directing you to the fish hatchery. Follow the winding road down to the Chattooga Picnic Area parking lot.*

The East Fork Trail, also known as the *hatchery trail*, has long been a favorite of hikers, campers and fishermen. This path is an absolute delight to walk as it parallels the tumbling East Fork of the Chattooga River down to its confluence with the "big" Chattooga. Take advantage of this scenic trail in conjunction with a trip to the hatchery and nearby picnic area for an entire day's worth of recreation.

This black-blazed trail begins in the Chattooga Picnic area along side the river and never strays far from the sound of rushing water. Dozens of tiny tributaries flow across the trail in their determined descent to the river, many featuring picturesque small waterfalls. Compared to other trails in the watershed,

The East Fork's "Forty Thousand Dollar Bridge"

The Chattooga Headwaters

the East Fork Trail has a remarkably gentle gradient as it methodically descends to the Chattooga River.

A massive and easily recognizable log bridge known as the *"Forty Thousand Dollar Bridge"* signals your upcoming arrival at the Chattooga River Trail junction. This area is shady and quite scenic, and is popular with campers and fishermen. It is not uncommon to see trout anglers, loaded with gear, heading along the trail coming to or from the river.

From the trail junction alongside the Chattooga, the Chattooga River Trail heads north for 1.8 miles to Ellicott Rock, and south for 2.1 equally scenic miles to Burrells Ford.

Fish Hatchery & Picnic Area
Ellicott Rock Wilderness, Sumter Natl. Forest, Oconee County, SC

Trail length: N/A - short walk
Difficulty: Easy
Elevation change: None
Features: Scenic picnic area, fish hatchery
USGS Quadrangle Map: Tamassee

Directions: *From Cashiers, follow Hwy 107 south for 11.7 miles (3.5 miles south of the state line) and turn right at the sign directing you to the fish hatchery. Follow the winding road down to the Chattooga Picnic Area parking lot.*

The Walhalla Fish Hatchery produces brook, brown and rainbow trout for stocking in local rivers and streams. Normally open to the public from 8 a.m. to 4 p.m., the hatchery is a fascinating place to visit. Large "raceways" are filled to the brim with fish destined for local streams. Children (and fishermen) will especially love to visit the hatchery.

Just across an East Fork footbridge, the Chattooga Picnic Area lies nestled beneath some of South Carolina's loftiest timber. The state's tallest white pine (165') and hemlock (148') can be found here. A number of picnic tables and a large rustic pavilion provide facilities for visitors.

Burrells Ford Primitive Camping Area
Sumter National Forest, Oconee County, SC

Directions: *From Cashiers, follow Hwy 107 south for approximately thirteen miles (approx. four miles south of the state line) to Burrells Ford Road (FS 708) on the right. Follow FS 708 for three miles to the campground parking area on the left, or continue 0.25 mile to the bridge. Burrells Ford Road is located approximately ten miles north of the Hwy 107 / Hwy 28 junction north of Walhalla.*

Burrells Ford Campground is a shady, somewhat secluded walk-in camping area tucked alongside a calm stretch of river several hundred yards downstream of busy Burrells Ford bridge. To reach the camping area requires about a 350 yard stroll - enough to discourage one from toting lots of heavy camping equipment.

Burrells Ford is definitely no frills, though a hand operated water pump and a pit toilet add a few touches of civilization. Several of the tent sites front tumbling King Creek which bisects the campground.

A lone angler above the Burrells Ford bridge

The campground is heavily used during the warmer months, especially during peak trout season. During these periods the Burrells Ford area can become quite a zoo, as fishermen line the banks and seemingly fill every available pool as they test their angling skills.

King Creek Falls
Sumter National Forest, Oconee County, SC

Trail length: 0.6 mile one way to falls
Difficulty: Easy
Elevation change: Approx. 200 feet
Features: Scenic waterfall
USGS Quadrangle Map: Tamassee

Directions: *See directions on previous page to the Burrells Ford Campground parking area. The path to the waterfall begins in the upper corner of the parking area behind the information board.*

One of the most inviting short hikes in the Chattooga headwaters region follows the combined Chattooga River & Foothills Trail to scenic King Creek Falls. This winning combination of an easy trail and a pretty waterfall make for a excellent short hiking destination.

From the parking area, follow the trail south for 0.4 mile to a narrow log bridge spanning rushing King Creek. Beyond, a trail sign directs hikers to the left, onto a spur trail which follows the small creek upstream. A several hundred yard uphill walk brings hikers to a narrow cove which surrounds the lovely eighty foot drop. A shallow pool at the base allows visitors to approach the splashing drop. Though not spectacular, King Creek Falls surprises first time visitors with its enjoyable sights and sounds.

King Creek Falls

The Long Trails of the Headwaters
The Bartram, Foothills & Chattooga River Trails
Sumter National Forest, Oconee County, SC

Trail length: Various lengths
Difficulty: Moderate
Elevation change: Generally several hundred feet
Features: Outstanding river scenery
USGS Quadrangle Map: Cashiers, Tamassee, Satolah

Directions: *See directions on previous page to the Burrells Ford Campground parking area. The path to the waterfall begins in the upper corner of the parking area behind the information board.*

The South Carolina side of the magnificent Chattooga features a network of river side trails extending from Ellicott Rock down to Russell bridge at Hwy 28. Portions of these trails closely parallel the river for 10.5 miles, rarely straying more than a few hundred yards from the water's edge. Both the Bartram and Foothills Trails eventually turn and head east away from the river, while the Chattooga River Trail continues south along the river to Hwy 28, reaching its current terminus twenty trail miles beyond at Hwy 76.

The first long segment worthy of note is the 7.3 mile portion of the Foothills Trail running from Sloan Bridge Picnic Area to Burrells Ford. This popular route intersects the hatchery road, effectively cutting this section of trail in half. The northern 3.4 miles covers a relatively easy route closely following the upper East Fork. The southern portion winds across the summit of rugged Medlin Mountain, reaching elevations in excess of 3,000 feet before dropping 600 feet into the Chattooga gorge. This segment intersects the Chattooga River Trail just south of Spoon Auger Falls, approximately 0.5 mile from the Burrells Ford Campground parking area.

North of the junction, the Chattooga River Trail runs 3.8 miles upstream to famed Ellicott Rock, providing hikers with a sensory overload of outstanding scenery. About half way from Burrells Ford to Ellicott Rock, the path reaches a junction with the East Fork Trail as it crosses the mammoth *"Forty Thousand Dollar Bridge."*

The most popular entrance point for this section is Burrells Ford Road (FS 708). Access the trail either at the eastern end of the bridge or in the campground parking area (allowing a side trip to King Creek Falls). Beyond the campground the two paths merge and continue downstream as the combined Chattooga River & Foothills Trail. Trail side scenery changes as quickly as the elevation, as the path undulates above the river. Broad, flat sections give way to steep rocky slopes. Sheer rock faces often crowd the trail. Dense rhododendron and laurel thickets alternate with lush beds of native ferns, making the trail a treat for the senses. Literally dozens of good primitive camping possibilities exist for hikers, though most seem to be located within a mile of Burrells Ford.

Approximately two miles below Burrells Ford the Chattooga negotiates a tight 180° bend aptly named *Big Bend*. Here a 2.7 mile side trail exits the corridor to the east, intersecting Hwy 107 just south of the Cherry Hill Campground. Big Bend Road (FS 709) parallels the path, and is usually only a few hundred yards to the north.

Below the Big Bend trail junction, the next segment of trail stretches 4.3 miles down to a point where the Bartram Trail exits the river corridor. This segment contains some of the most scenic hiking along the entire river, and begins with a steady ascent of Round Top Mountain. Only 0.5 mile below Big Bend,

Rugged cascade below Big Bend

an ominous roar heralds Big Bend Falls, one of several major drops along the upper Chattooga. This impressive waterfall plunges almost 20 vertical feet over a broken ledge. A tricky descent along the steep, overgrown river bank provides a view of the waterfall. Use extreme care here, as the rocks around the base are spray-soaked and usually very slippery.

One noteworthy portion of this section occurs as the trail is forced to the edge of the riverbed by intrusive rocks and cliffs. Though not a problem at normal levels, high water could mean some portions of the trail could be under some shallow water. Many scenic cascades occur regularly along the trail, often followed by inviting sandy beaches. The more scenic beaches usually have primitive camping areas close by.

Approximately two miles below Big Bend Falls, another sharp U-turn in the river heralds the foreboding Rock Gorge, a rugged canyon where the river drops over 100 vertical feet in slightly over one mile. The main trail skirts the edge of the gorge high above the river before continuing one additional mile down to the junction where the Bartram Trail enters the river corridor. *(Only the most experienced hikers should attempt to enter Rock Gorge, as sheer cliffs and steep rock faces make exploring the river both difficult and dangerous.)*

The Bartram Trail enters via a 2.3 mile section that stretches southeast to Hwy 107, eventually reaching Oconee State Park nearly six miles south. Another convenient Bartram Trail access point is located 0.5 mile from the river along Nicholson Ford Road near Thrift Lake.

The newly combined Bartram & Chattooga River Trail continues south along the river. This final leg winds 3.7 serene miles down to Russell Bridge at Hwy 28. One major attraction is encountered right off the bat - two pretty cascades along picturesque Lick Log Creek. Beyond is a relatively uneventful yet highly enjoyable 3.5 mile walk to the bridge. The initial 1.5 miles closely parallels the Chattooga, while the final two miles climb along a low ridge before descending into a broad valley. This portion of the trail ends at Ridley Fields on the east side of Russell bridge.

Reed Creek Bottoms and Gorge
Chattahoochee National Forest, Rabun County, Georgia

Trail length: Approx. 1.8 miles one way to Reed Creek
Difficulty: Easy
Elevation change: Minimal
Features: Chattooga scenery
USGS Quadrangle Map: Satolah

Directions: *From US Hwy 441 in Clayton, turn onto Warwoman Road (next to the Days Inn) and proceed 13.7 miles to the stop sign. Turn right onto Hwy 28 and drive 2.2 miles to Russell bridge.*

For those adventurers who would like to get off the often busy major headwaters trails, a trip to Reed Creek Bottoms might be a good choice. Several hundred yards north of the Hwy 28 bridge, an old gated logging road shortcuts a large bend in the river and comes along side the Chattooga approximately 1.2 miles from the highway.

The path narrows as it reaches the river, closely following the Chattooga until it reaches the broad, flat floodplain (known as a "bottom") at Reed Creek. Much of this area has been planted in loblolly pine, and the combination of tall grasses and shady pines make the area open and inviting.

Along the river bank at Reed Creek Bottoms

Noisy Reed Creek flows along the eastern flank of the bottoms and enters the Chattooga rather uneventfully. This entire portion of the river is quite placid, and has long been popular with fishermen. Several old paths cut through heavy underbrush across the bottoms heading north. These paths converge and follow an old roadbed up to the mouth of rugged Reed Creek gorge.

Further up the gorge, remnants of old paths make hiking tolerable at best, though surveyors tape suggest that improved trails are in the works here. Use caution exploring the area as it it is isolated and contains rough, steep, overgrown terrain. While it is possible to hike up the creek for about two miles to Persimmon Gap on Burrells Ford Road, this trip would require a tremendous amount of bushwhacking.

From Reed Creek Bottoms, an alternate route back to the bridge is available. Veer to the left across a wildlife clearing south of the bottoms and follow the riverside trail along the remnants of an old overgrown roadbed. While this route is longer, it does provide some good access points along the river. Be sure to follow the roadbed (path) as it angles away from the river and hugs the western slopes of Brack Hill. If you try to go all the way to the bridge along the river you will encounter one of the worst patches of briars and thick undergrowth in the Southern Appalachians. Several publications list a path here, but it is long overgrown and nearly impassable. Be sure to take a good look at the beaver pond and marsh along the west side of the bridge.

The CHATTOOGA
Wild and Scenic River

3

Section I
The West Fork

The free-falling West Fork roars down a rugged canyon several hundred yards below Three Forks.

40   *The Chattooga Wild and Scenic River*

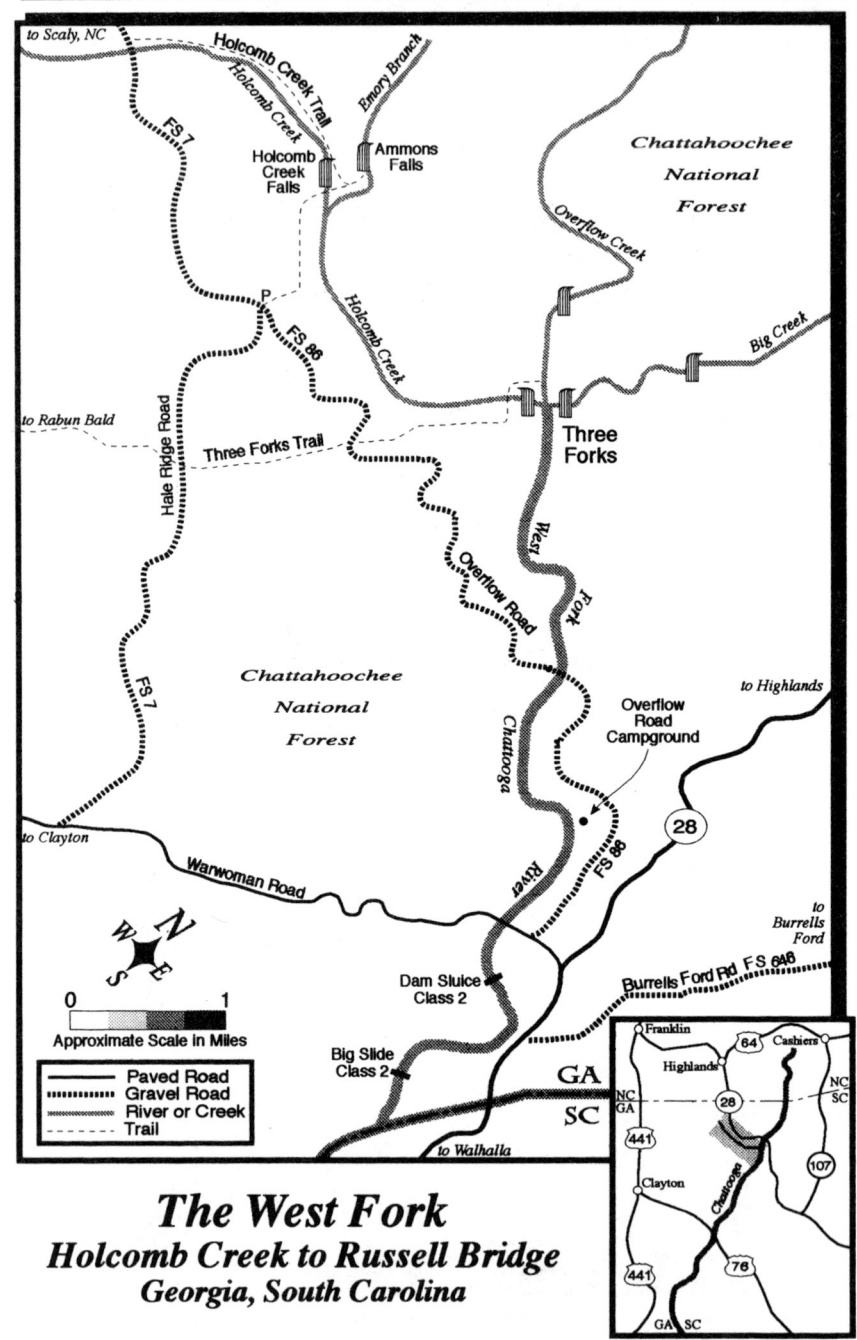

The West Fork
Holcomb Creek to Russell Bridge
Georgia, South Carolina

Section I - The West Fork

Three Forks to The Chattooga River

Rugged backcountry scenery and gentle whitewater

The Chattooga's West Fork has a very special birthplace, formed at the junction of three beautiful mountain streams. This rugged river then flows southeast through Georgia's Rabun County in the beautiful Chattahoochee National Forest. The total length of the West Fork from its birth to its confluence with the Chattooga is seven miles, with the lower four miles suitable for novice paddlers or even inner tubes.

Foot travel is difficult in this rough backcountry area, though several points of interest have good trail access. Fishing is a prime attraction along the West Fork, and trout fishermen by the scores visit both the upper and lower West Fork, as well as its parent tributaries - Big, Overflow and Holcomb Creeks.

The lower West Fork is easily accessible as it winds within close proximity to both Overflow Road and Highway 28, though visitors must be aware that portions of the river run through private property - please respect "no trespassing" signs. The West Fork doesn't have the pounding whitewater of the lower Chattooga, but its watershed contains many worthy destinations.

Floating The West Fork
Overflow Road to Long Bottom Ford

The West Fork of the Chattooga River offers boaters and tubers approximately four miles of easy, scenic floating suitable for just about any skill level. The current along this portion of the river is moderate to slow, and the width of the stream averages about 30 - 50 feet.

A shady canopy of forest leans out over much of the

stream along its slow journey down to main river, enveloping floaters in welcome shade. Numerous other portions of the river traverse broad, open stretches, providing glimpses of the surrounding valley.

Perhaps the most popular put-in is at Overflow Road Campground. Here the carry to the river is short and flat. Downstream of the camping area and Warwoman Road bridge, only occasional small shoals break up an otherwise placid float. None of these shoals exceed an easy Class II rating, though two are deemed worthy of a name - *Dam Sluice* and *Big Slide*.

The takeout for West Fork floaters is at Long Bottom Ford, approximately one mile below the confluence of the West Fork with the Chattooga. A paved boat ramp adjacent to the parking area makes removal from the river fairly easy - something boaters on the other sections of the river cannot enjoy.

West Fork Access Points for Boaters

Warwoman Road Bridge: *From US Hwy 441 in Clayton, turn onto Warwoman Road (next to Days Inn) and proceed 13.5 miles to the bridge over the West Fork. Be sure to park well off the road and heed any parking signs.*

Overflow Road Campground: *Follow the directions above. Just beyond the West Fork bridge, turn left onto Overflow Road (FS 86) and proceed approximately one mile to the camping area on the left.*

Long Bottom Ford: *Follow the directions to Warwoman bridge. Instead of turning left onto Overflow Road, continue east on Warwoman for just a few hundred yards to the stop sign at Hwy 28. Turn right and proceed 2.2 miles to Russell Bridge and the GA / SC state line. Continue straight ahead for 1.3 miles to the Long Bottom Ford boat launch area on the right.*

Paddling The West Fork - General Information

Gradient:	10 feet per mile
Width:	30 - 50 feet
Length:	4 miles
Seasons:	year round
Acceptable levels:	Minimum 0.5 feet
	Maximum 3.5 feet

Gauge is located at Russell Bridge on Highway 28.

Exploring The West Fork on Foot

Holcomb Creek Trail
Chattahoochee National Forest, Rabun County, Georgia

Trail length: 0.6 mile one way or 1.6 mile loop
Difficulty: Moderate
Elevation change: Approx. 200 feet (400 feet for loop)
Features: Two beautiful waterfalls, scenic streams
USGS Quadrangle Map: Rabun Bald

Directions: *From US Hwy 441 in Clayton, turn onto Warwoman Road (next to Days Inn) and proceed seven miles to Hale Ridge Road (FS 7) on the left. Follow Hale Ridge Road for 6.8 miles to the intersection of Hale Ridge and Overflow Road (FS 86). Park here. The trailhead is on the north side of the intersection.*

Though several miles from the West Fork, one of the most enjoyable hikes to be found in this area is the Holcomb Creek Trail, featuring two scenic waterfalls just a short walk from the trailhead. Beautiful Holcomb Creek appears about 0.4 mile below the trailhead. This spectacular cascade spills 120 feet over a rugged rock face before rushing beneath a wooden bridge spanning the creek. This bridge provides an excellent vantage point from which to view and photograph the cascade.

Beyond the falls the trail continues flat, then begins a steady 0.2 mile climb (passing a spur trail on the left) to a dead-end on an observation platform with a close-up view of Ammons Creek Falls. Here Ammons Creek (or *Emory Creek* as it is listed on many maps) spills over a steep rock face just yards from the platform. The total drop at Ammons Creek Falls is about 40 feet. While not spectacular, it is still highly scenic and well worth the visit.

Visitors may retrace their steps 0.6 mile back to the trailhead or follow the spur trail below Ammons Creek Falls *uphill* along cascading Holcomb Creek for 0.5 mile to its junction with Hale Ridge Road. To complete the loop, walk back down Hale Ridge Road 0.6 mile to the original trailhead. The total loop distance is about 1.6 miles. Either route you take, it's hard to go wrong on this trail.

Three Forks Trail
Chattahoochee National Forest, Rabun County, Georgia

Trail length: 1.25 to Holcomb Cr; 1.5 miles to Three Forks
Difficulty: Mod. to Holcomb Cr; *Difficult* to Three Forks
Elevation change: Approx. 500 feet
Features: Waterfalls, Three Forks, West Fork
USGS Quadrangle Map: Satolah
Note: *The hike to Three Forks is not suitable for children.*

Directions: *From US Hwy 441 in Clayton, turn onto Warwoman Road (next to Days Inn) and proceed 13.5 miles to Overflow Road (FS 86) on the left. Turn here and drive four miles to John Teague Gap. There is a small parking area on the right and a sign marking the trailhead.*

Rabun County's *Three Forks Trail* offers one of the most varied outdoor experiences to be found in the Southeast. On this trail's western end rises mighty Rabun Bald, almost 4,700' above sea level, while the eastern terminus is enticingly close to the rugged West Fork, nearly 9.5 miles distant and 3,000 vertical feet below. The only real problem with this trail, besides being very challenging, is that it doesn't run *all the way* to *Three Forks*. It has everything an experienced hiker longs for - isolation, scenery, wildlife - but actually reaching *Three Forks* can be frustrating and even dangerous.

Novice hikers should stick with the 1.25 mile walk to the trail's junction with Holcomb Creek. This area features a scenic portion of the creek, and provides a glimpse of a powerful cascade just downstream. From the parking area at John Teague Gap, follow the white-blazed trail east along a high ridgeline. At approximately one mile, the trail intersects an old logging road. Turn left here and walk downhill to rushing Holcomb Creek. Use caution, as the creek has several steep, slippery drop-offs around the cascade. Upstream, fishermen and hikers alike will enjoy a string of crystalline pools along Holcomb Creek. This is the end of the line for casual hiking though.

To reach *Three Forks* is somewhat difficult from this point. If you have any doubts, look at a USGS topo map for the area. All those pretty little lines squeezed together add up to a difficult, scrambling descent in order to reach the famous junction. This is one of the steepest areas in the Chattooga region, so use caution! Perhaps the most popular route from the Holcomb Creek crossing involves looking for the faint path on the far side of the creek that (roughly) follows the general direction of the creek toward *Three Forks*. Several overgrown paths emerge along Overflow Creek just above the forks. Some visitors choose to pick and climb down alongside tumbling Holcomb Creek. Either way is about one-quarter mile, and both routes are hard and dirty. *Watch out for numerous steep drop-offs in this area!*

Yet another possibility involves backtracking to the one mile point where the trail intersects the jeep road. Instead of turning left, head to the right, following a faint path to the northeast. This path plummets to the river just a few hundred yards below *Three Forks*. Once alongside the river, hikers can pick their way back upstream toward the famous junction.

Three Forks as seen from small falls on Holcomb Creek

Section I - The West Fork

Despite the obstacles, *Three Forks* is a very worthy destination. Here the West Fork is born at the near right-angle junction of three sizable streams - Holcomb, Overflow and Big Creeks. Holcomb Creek and Big Creek enter the junction over sparkling small waterfalls. Not to be outdone, Overflow Creek features its own waterfall several hundred yards upstream. Other noteworthy cascades occur upstream along Big Creek.

Huge boulders and sheer bluffs create an imposing wilderness setting which is hard to find in the populous Southeast. Getting around the area is hard work and can be dangerous to the careless, but *Three Forks* offers great rewards for those up to the challenge.

Note: Many visitors prefer to access Three Forks from the east via a system of roads and trails from Hwy 28. Please refer to current topo maps or contact the Forest Service for more information.

Overflow Road Primitive Camping Area
Chattahoochee National Forest, Rabun County, Georgia

Directions: *From US Hwy 441 in Clayton, turn onto Warwoman Road (next to Days Inn) and proceed 13.5 miles to Overflow Road (FS 86) on the left. Turn here and proceed one mile to Overflow Road Camping Area on the left.*

The small primitive camping area along Overflow Road provides a good option for those visitors who wish to camp close to the river *and* still have easy access to their vehicles. Secluded and primitive, this camping area lies nestled along the flat riverbank in one of the few "official" camping areas in the river corridor. A pit toilet is about the only modern convenience you will find here.

Though visitors may be fortunate enough to have the camping area all to themselves during the off-season, warm weather weekends, particularly during hunting or trout fishing seasons, often find the camping area full.

The CHATTOOGA
Wild and Scenic River

4

Section II

One of the many easy ledges along scenic Section II.

50   *The Chattooga Wild and Scenic River*

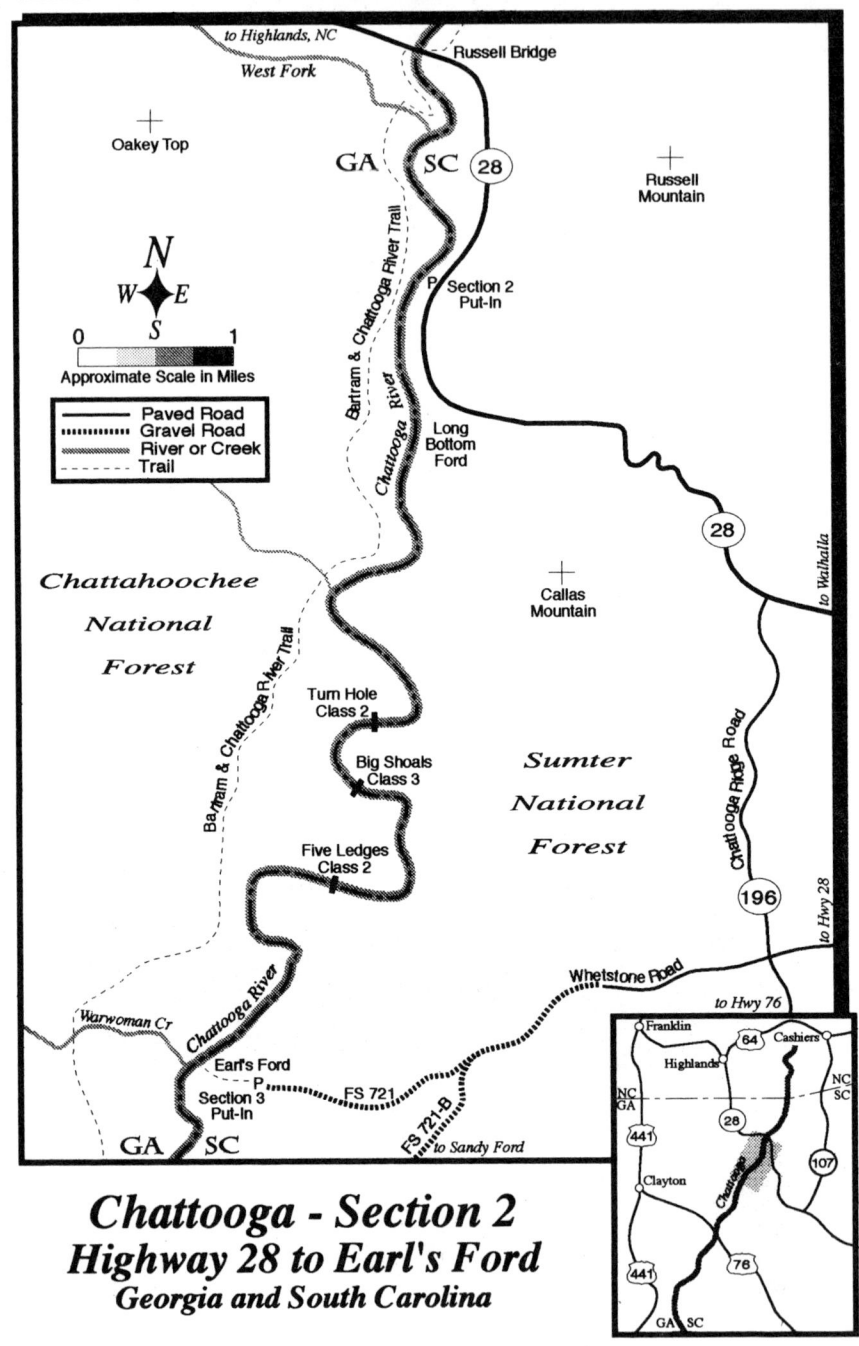

Chattooga - Section 2
Highway 28 to Earl's Ford
Georgia and South Carolina

Section II

Long Bottom Ford to Earl's Ford

Ideal paddling for the novice whitewater boater.

Section II of the Chattooga offers an ideal setting for novice boaters. Though much of its seven mile course is flat and calm, numerous easy shoals and one tricky Class III make Section II a great whitewater classroom for the beginner. The unbeatable combination of gorgeous scenery and easy whitewater make this stretch of the Chattooga popular with paddlers of every skill level.

Though only one developed trail currently exists - the combined **Bartram & Chattooga River Trail**, it provides access to plenty of splendid scenery. When planning your visit to Chattooga Country, don't overlook the recreational opportunities that Section II has to offer.

Floating Section II
Long Bottom Ford to Earl's Ford

Section II is an ideal training run for beginning whitewater boaters, and has ample scenery to attract experienced boaters as well. Seven miles of beautiful mountain ambience peppered with lively Class II and III whitewater make this an attractive year-round run.

Downstream of the launching ramp at the Long Bottom Ford parking area, the initial two miles run somewhat narrow and slow, interrupted only by an occasional small shoal. The river winds peacefully through a wide valley, and thick streamside growth shields paddlers from much of the noise from nearby Hwy 28. This uppermost portion of the valley was once heavily farmed. Prior to the first white settlers, a major Indian settlement existed here. This area, once busy with activity, is slowly returning to its original forested condition. The remains of the old Russell farm still stand, but not much else other than a few seasonal riverside cabins along a small stretch of private land near Long Bottom Ford.

At the end of the valley, the personality of the river begins to change, as the Chattooga begins to reclaim its wilderness identity. The channel widens and shallows, and the pace definitely quickens a bit. Lively shoals become more numerous, and the first Class II deemed worthy of a name is encountered - *Turn Hole*. There are numerous routes through this series of small drops, so take your time and experiment if you are new to the sport of whitewater paddling. This is one of those areas where you can begin developing the water-reading skills you will need in more difficult whitewater.

One-half mile further downstream a large boulder pile seems to be blocking the river. This is *Big Shoals*, the only Class III on Section II. Stop along the rock pile in mid-river and scout this rapid. The most popular route here is to the right of the scouting rock, a choice which requires some technical maneuvering in swift water. At higher water levels another route appears to the left of the scouting rock. Whichever way

An Unconventional Watercraft tackles Section II's *Big Shoals*

Early morning scene from the beach at Earl's Ford

you choose, it is an easy portage over the rock pile if you decide to run the drop again. *Big Shoals* is a fairly forgiving rapid, as a large recovery pool forms below the drop to catch dunked paddlers. The rockpile in mid-river is a popular lunch spot, and the pool below creates an inviting place for a swim.

The remaining few miles of Section II offer up long, placid pools interspersed with lively Class I and II shoals. The scenery remains excellent throughout the remainder of the run. A large overhanging rock along the left bank signals your proximity to Earl's Ford, the end of Section II. This is also the end of the Chattooga's easy water. A large, well-trodden beach on the left marks the end of Section II paddling and the beginning of the worst part of the trip - the arduous quarter-mile uphill haul to your vehicle.

Section II Access Points for Boaters

Warwoman Road Bridge: *From US Hwy 441 in Clayton, turn onto Warwoman Road (next to Days Inn) and proceed 13.7 miles to the intersection with Hwy 28. Turn right and proceed 2.2 miles to Russell Bridge and the GA / SC state line. Continue straight ahead for 1.3 miles to the Long Bottom Ford boat launch area on the right.*

Earl's Ford: *From Long Bottom Ford, follow Hwy 28 south for 4.4 miles to Chattooga Ridge Road on the right. Proceed 3.4 miles to the four-way stop sign. Turn right and follow Earl's Ford Road to the end of the pavement. The road then becomes FS 721. Proceed straight ahead for approximately two miles to the parking area at the end of the road.*

From Clayton, Take US Hwy 76 east for nine miles, crossing into South Carolina over the Chattooga River. Continue 2.1 miles to Chattooga Ridge Road on the left. Turn here and proceed 5.8 miles to the four-way stop sign. Turn left onto Earl's Ford Road and follow it approximately 3.5 miles to the Earl's Ford parking area at the end of the road.

Paddling Section II - General Information

Gradient:	12 feet per mile
Width:	25 - 100 feet
Length:	7 miles
Seasons:	year round
Acceptable levels:	Minimum 0.8 feet
	Maximum 3.5 feet

Gauge is located at Russell Bridge on Hwy 28.

Exploring Section II on Foot

Bartram & Chattooga River Trail
Chattahoochee National Forest, Rabun County, Georgia

Trail length: Russell bridge to Sandy Ford - 10 miles
Difficulty: Moderate
Elevation change: Approx. 200 feet
Features: Forest scenery, river vistas
USGS Quadrangle Map: Satolah, Whetstone; copy of the Forest Service Chattooga River map suggested.

Directions: *From US Hwy 441 in Clayton, turn onto Warwoman Road (next to Days Inn) and proceed 13.7 miles to the stop sign. Turn right onto Hwy 28 and drive 2.2 miles to Russell bridge.*

To reach the Sandy Ford trailhead, take Warwoman Road from Clayton for 5.7 miles. Turn right onto Sandy Ford Road. Proceed 0.65 mile, then turn left, crossing a small bridge, and proceed 4 miles (fording Dick's Creek twice) to the Bartram Trail crossing marked by a large boulder. Several hundred yards to the north the Bartram Trail joins the Chattooga River Trail and heads to the north toward Russell bridge. To the west, the Bartram Trail winds toward Warwoman Dell. (At the second ford, if the creek is high, park here and walk downstream along the creek about 0.4 mile to a junction with the Bartram & Chattooga River Trail.)

The well-known Bartram & Chattooga River Trail roughly follows the western bank of the Chattooga southwest from Russell bridge for 10 scenic miles. The trail splits just west of Sandy Ford near a convenient trailhead along the upper reaches of the Chattooga's Section III. This path follows white diamond-shaped blazes along a moderate course which features a great deal of forest hiking and relatively little river contact.

This section of the trail originates at Russell Bridge, and winds sidewalk flat southwest for 0.25 mile before turning north and following the West Fork up to a wet ford. This crossing may be waist-deep under some conditions, so use caution. Do not attempt to ford the river if it is cloudy and you can not see the bottom! This crossing occurs only yards from *Big Slide*, one of the West Fork's lively Class II rapids.

The next three miles closely parallel the river, often passing within view of the sparkling stream. At points along the trail, beautiful vistas of the surrounding valley become visible. The path crosses Adline Branch at the southern end of the Long Bottom Ford area. The next two miles are spent alternately climbing and descending as the path angles away from the river. The 5 mile mark is reached at a crossing of Laurel Branch, and begins a series of twisting turns along the base of 2,417' Willis Knob.

Over the next mile the pathway descends to Warwoman Creek, a major Chattooga tributary. Another wet fording is required, this one usually about knee-deep. The trail then crosses Earl's Ford Road before continuing alongside the creek for approximately one-quarter mile. As the trail leaves the creek, it turns southwest toward the Chattooga once more, intersecting the river about 0.5 mile below Warwoman Creek.

The Bartram & Chattooga River Trail closely follows the river for nearly 0.5 mile, angling away near the vicinity of the river's noteworthy *Rock Garden* area, along the northern end of Section III. A fairly short (off-trail) detour will reveal dozens of huge granite boulders and slabs projecting from the riverbed. This area is one of the river's most scenic areas.

Approximately 0.5 mile beyond, the path crosses Dick's Creek. A short side trail follows the river down to Dick's Creek Falls. This scenic cascade drops about 50 feet down a smooth rock face directly into the river opposite mammoth *Dick's Creek Ledge*, a Class IV Chattooga rapid. The view from the area alongside the top of the waterfall is alone worth the hike. This is truly a spot to savor.

South of the Dick's Creek Falls spur trail, the Bartram & Chattooga River Trail continues south for 0.5 mile before splitting into two separate trails. The Bartram Trail heads west toward Warwoman Dell, while the Chattooga River Trail continues southwest, crossing Sandy Ford Road just a few hundred yards from the end of the road at Sandy Ford. The Chattooga River Trail then continues southwest to its current terminus at Hwy 76, some ten miles distant.

From the trail split, the Bartram Trail travels west for several hundred yards to Sandy Ford Road. Here a large inscribed boulder marks the crossing, while a cleared area alongside the road provides spaces to park several cars.

Exploring Section II by Hoof

Willis Knob - Rocky Gap Horse Camp & Trails
Chattahoochee National Forest, Rabun County, Georgia
Sumter National Forest, Oconee County, South Carolina

Directions: *From US Hwy 441 in Clayton, turn onto Warwoman Road (next to Days Inn) and proceed 11 miles to Goldmine Road (FS 157) on the right. Follow FS 157 for 0.2 mile to the Woodall Ridge Day Use parking area or 1.9 miles to Willis Knob Horse Camp.*

The Rocky Gap - Willis Knob Horse Camp features 27.5 miles of great horseback riding and sublime mountain scenery. Located along Section II, the *RGWK* trails cross the Chattooga from Georgia into South Carolina, and include scenic portions of both the Chattahoochee and Sumter National Forests.

A number of excellent trails offer loops of various lengths, and three Chattooga River fords provide some extra excitement. These river crossings are easily passable at normal water levels, but the Forest Service recommends the ford at **Adline Branch as the safest.**

On the Georgia side of the River, the *Willis Knob Horse Camp* is available by reservation. This facility consists of eight sites. Reservations must be made in advance by contacting:

Tallulah Ranger District
P.O. Box 438
Clayton, GA 30525
(706) 782-3320

South Carolina's *Whetstone Base Camp* can also be reserved in advance. Unreserved sites will be issued on a first-come basis. Reservations and additional information may be obtained from:

Andrew Pickens Ranger District
112 Andrew Pickens Circle
Mountain Rest, SC 29664
(864) 638-9568

The Forest Service has an informational brochure on the RGWK trails and facilities which includes a map of the trails and complete reservations information. Contact one of the above addresses for additional information.

The CHATTOOGA
Wild and Scenic River

5

Section III

Magnificent scenery at Section III's Bull Sluice.

60 *The Chattooga Wild and Scenic River*

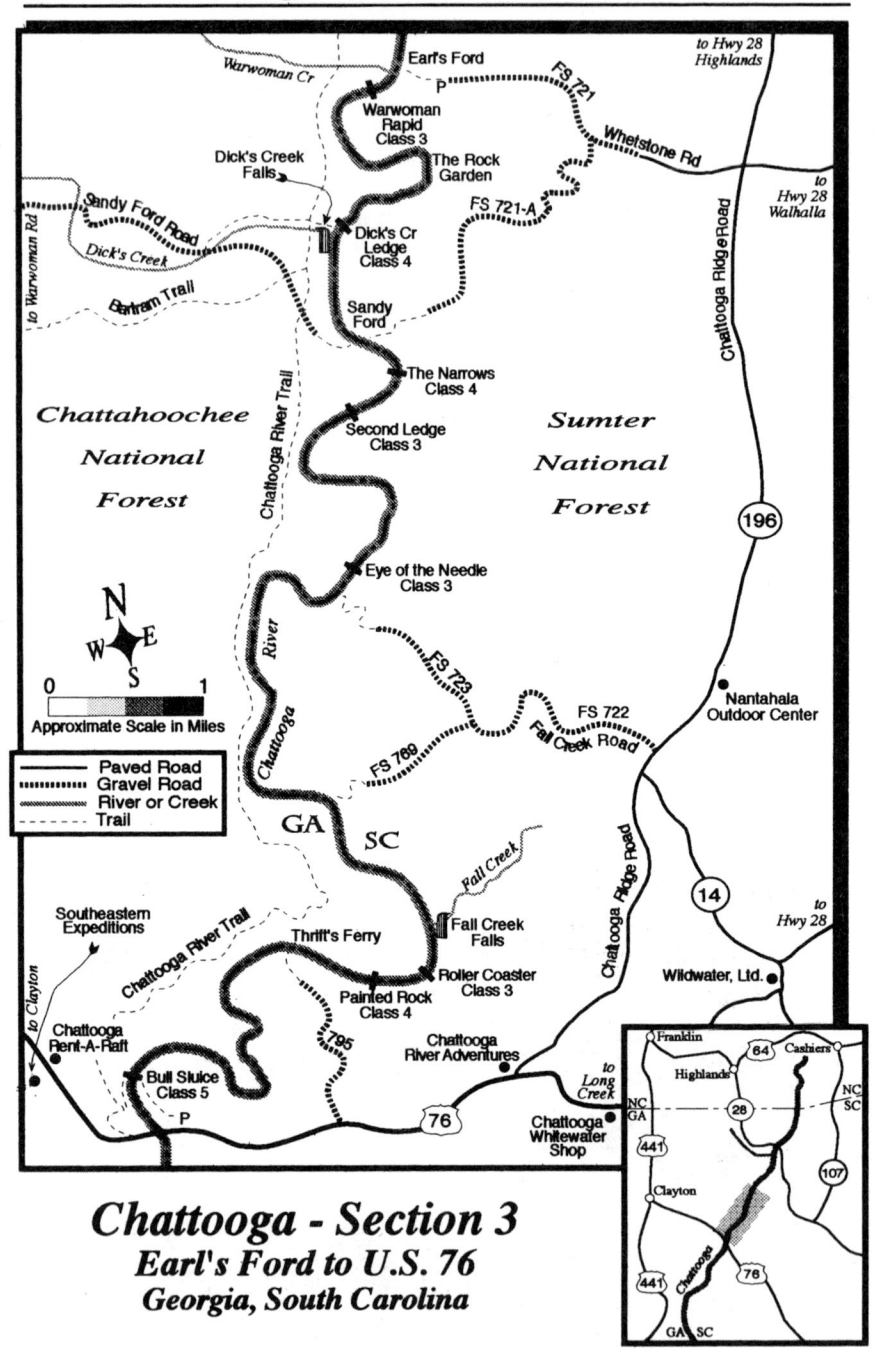

Chattooga - Section 3
Earl's Ford to U.S. 76
Georgia, South Carolina

Section III

Earl's Ford to US Hwy 76

The ideal river for the open boater.

Section III of the Chattooga River features 13 delightful miles - from Earl's Ford on the north to the Hwy 76 bridge southeast of Clayton. Whitewater enthusiasts fall in love with Section III's stunningly beautiful scenery and challenging whitewater, reaching a Class V crescendo at Bull Sluice rapid. Section III is much more difficult than either the West Fork or Section II. The current is stronger, the rapids much more numerous and challenging, and access somewhat limited. Only intermediate or advanced paddlers should attempt Section III.

Access to the river on foot comes mainly via Forest Service roads leading to the edge of the river corridor. Several nice short hikes lead to beautiful river scenery. The parking area on the South Carolina side of Hwy 76 is a good place to start, as several information boards contain various facts and tidbits about the river. From here visitors can easily access a scenic stretch of river and giant Bull Sluice rapid. For those looking for longer excursions into the wilderness, the Chattooga River Trail winds along the western edge of the corridor from Sandy Ford down to Hwy 76.

Floating Section III

Earl's Ford to Sandy Ford - Mile 0.0 to Mile 3.0

Section III of the Chattooga officially kicks-off at Earl's Ford, though the journey really starts at the parking area one-quarter mile to the east. Here boaters must shoulder fully-equipped canoes, kayaks or rafts and begin the arduous carry -thankfully downhill - to the sandy beach at Earl's Ford. Registration is accomplished at the information board located by the trail head leading down to the beach. Floating the entire thirteen miles of Section III can take all day, so get on the river early, and allow yourself plenty of time.

Section III has often been referred to as the ideal river for open canoes, while still presenting plenty of excitement for decked boats. This reputation is well deserved, and first-timers find out early on why boaters come here from all over the country.

There is plenty of scenery and excitement right from the start, as sneaky Class III *Warwoman Rapid* is encountered just a few hundred yards downstream of the put-in. If you have trouble negotiating this twisting drop, it would be best to paddle back upstream and take out, as things will only get a lot worse (or better, depending upon your skill level) from here.

One mile downstream of Earl's Ford the Chattooga enters one of the more scenic portions of Section III - the *Rock Garden*. Granite slabs embedded in the river jut out like huge fingers, towering over paddlers as they negotiate the garden. Take your time and meander through this unusual area. Several small but lively chutes must be tackled, so don't get too caught up in the scenery and forget about the river.

Below the *Rock Garden*, the river widens and slows. Just downstream an ominous roar forewarns

Dick's Creek Ledge & Falls

paddlers of the first major drop of the day - *Dick's Creek Ledge* (aka *First Ledge*). Look for rocks in mid-river which form a definite horizon line. Land here to scout the drop.

From the rocks, paddlers will also be treated to an outstanding view of *Dick's Creek Falls* (aka Five Finger Falls). This unusual 50 foot waterfall is formed as Dick's Creek flows over a smooth granite face directly into the river at the base of the river-wide ledge. The unique combination of a wild waterfall, thundering whitewater and the surrounding mountains make this one of the most beautiful scenes on the river.

To successfully run Class IV *Dick's Creek Ledge* requires a strong *S*-maneuver over a double drop. Run to the left of the scouting rock. This drop becomes more difficult as the river level rises, as paddlers must drop over the first curved ledge, then turn abruptly right and hit a narrow but powerful chute which rushes to the base of the ledge. Here, a quick left turn is required. One good thing about this intimidating rapid is the easy portage over the ledge. Do it quickly while everyone is sight-seeing and maybe no one will notice.

Several hundred yards downstream, head to the left of two small, wooded islands (the right channel may be blocked by a dangerous log jam) and run the *Stairsteps*, a fun series of Class III whitewater. Keep your eyes open for downed trees in this area - *if any are sighted, keep well away*- they can create hazardous strainers which can trap boaters. The *Stairsteps* spit paddlers out into an extended pool bordered on the Georgia side by a sandy beach. This area is appropriately named Sandy Ford, and is a popular local fishing hole, swimming beach, and place for locals to party. Unfortunately, Rabun County allows vehicles access to the beach here, and the result has been a great deal of erosion and plenty of unsightly trash. If visiting this area from the Georgia side, please help to preserve this area by parking your vehicle well up the road away from the river.

On the South Carolina side, several short trails wind up to the Sandy Ford parking area on FS 721A. This area provides access for running only a portion of Section III. The shuttle back to Earl's Ford should only take 10 minutes or so.

Floating Section III
Sandy Ford to Fall Creek Road - Mile 3.0 to Mile 8.0

Below Sandy Ford, the river gains momentum and spills over several small ledges and shoals. The next broad left bend brings paddlers to a large pool at the top of the *Narrows*, one of Section III's most intimidating rapids. Beach on the left and walk downstream to scout the top of this drop. This 150 yard long Class IV is somewhat complex. The upper half offers a long series of ledges which funnel down in width. Below the initial drop, the river bends to the right and features several big holes and a few powerful waves. The current is very strong and unpredictable.

The most popular route through the upper section is toward the right-center, but several paths are possible. The *Narrows* is really spectacular above 2.5' as exploding waves spray mist into the canyon air. Below the initial 75 yards or so, the river narrows drastically, creating fierce currents. All the rocks in the riverbed are extremely undercut and therefore very dangerous. It's a good idea to have an experienced boater lead the way and set up throw ropes.

The Upper portion of the Narrows

Near the base of the rapid the Chattooga squeezes through a 10 foot wide slot between boulders, emptying into an emerald green pool with sheer rock walls to the left and huge house-sized boulders to the right. This is arguably the most beautiful single spot on the river. The currents remain strong, even in the pool, and the rocks downstream are severely undercut. There is no good practical way to portage the *Narrows*, so be sure of your boating skills and take all precautions. This is not a good place to find yourself out of your boat.

The exciting Class III drop at Second Ledge

Below the *Narrows*, the Chattooga widens considerably and resumes a more moderate pace, but not for long. Several hundred yards downstream is *Second Ledge*, the most dramatic Class III rapid on the river. This heart-pounding six foot vertical drop can be scouted from the left bank or the rock pile near mid-river. To run the ledge, head straight over the falls just yards from the South Carolina bank, though the exact spot may vary depending on the water level. Several strategically placed rocks near the brink can upset your balance. Get up a good head of steam and prepare to brace in the highly aerated water at the base of the ledge. *Second Ledge* is famous for flipping novice boaters, so beware!

Below *Second Ledge* is a well deserved two mile stretch of easy Class I and II shoals dripping in magnificent scenery. Paddlers should take this opportunity to rest from the adrenaline rush just past and enjoy the relaxed pace. *Eye-of-the-Needle* is the next noteworthy rapid. This fast, narrow Class III chute is run against the far left bank. A large boulder pile extending from the right bank announces your approach. Scout from the right bank. To run this tricky chute, follow the tongue down along the far left bank and into the chute. The current will hurl you toward a large boulder on the bank, but normally pushes you to the right, away from the rock, at just the last moment. More than a few paddlers and their boats have become attached, so to speak, to this rock over the years. It never hurts to possess a good draw stroke.

Section III Action

Eye-of-the-Needle is the last moderate action for several miles. The stretch of river below the rapid is somewhat slow, and offers up more great views. The steady current and relative absence of shoals makes this a good area to relax and just float. Keep your eyes open, as this area is a good spot to catch wildlife, especially deer, in the river.

After a prolonged straight stretch of nearly one mile, the river bends sharply left and spills over an extended series of small drops down to a broad pool with a small beach on the South Carolina bank. Look for a vertical log with *"Fall Creek Trail"* carved into it. A steep, winding 0.3 mile path winds up to a small parking area at the end of FS 769, a Fall Creek Road spur.

Though eight miles of Section III have passed since Earl's Ford, nearly another 5 miles remains before the Hwy 76 bridge. If the water is low, boaters often either take-out here or use this trail as the put-in and run the lower portion of Section III.

Floating Section III
Fall Creek Road to US Hwy 76 - Mile 8.0 to Mile 12.5

Below the Fall Creek Trail, the river is fairly serene offering only a few small shoals. Approximately 0.6 mile downstream, scenic stair stepping Fall Creek Falls tumbles into the river on the South Carolina side. This pretty little cascade is a pleasant spot for a break. Decked boaters sometimes plunge from the rocks around the falls directly into the river (*not recommended*).

Several hundred yards ahead, the river narrows into a series of standing waves known as *Roller Coaster*. The higher the water level, the more exciting the ride in this rodeo-like Class III. The best way to tackle *Roller Coaster* is to get up a good head of steam and plow up over the tops of the waves. Boaters who take on a bit of water will have a placid stretch just ahead in which to bail out or recover.

Several hundred yards ahead the river bends sharply right and enters *Painted Rock* (aka *Keyhole*), a tricky Class IV. Stop at the beach on the left and walk down to scout. *Painted Rock* is composed of a series of ledges which funnel down onto a large undercut rock. Boaters usually begin their run near the center of the river and angle right. Stay away from the large rock at the base - a tremendous amount of water flushes beneath it. If by chance your boat broaches the rock, lean *downstream* and climb onto it.

Section III Action

Three more scenic miles of mild whitewater remain, including a Class II-III drop known as *Hound's Tooth* about one mile below *Painted Rock*. Enjoy the relative calm, but pay close attention. When the river sweeps through a broad left bend, begin heading to the right bank. Below the bend, the Chattooga is choked by a massive boulder pile extending from the Georgia bank. Beach in one of the small pools along the right bank and walk downstream to scout famous *Bull Sluice*, the first of the Chattooga's Class V monsters. The ominous roar from down river should be enough to ensure that you stop and scout (good idea).

Bull Sluice plunges over a series of two back-to-back drops for a total descent of about twelve feet. The initial drop is over a curved ledge into a pool of powerful cross-currents. A strong hydraulic at the base of the first drop can easily flip boats. The flow then funnels wildly between the boulder pile and a large overhanging (at low water) rock known affectionately as "*Decapitation Rock*." This concentrated chute of aerated water then explodes downward out of the rapid into a large recovery pool.

Riding the Bull

Just lining up to run the *Bull* takes a good degree of whitewater skill. The entrance rapids above *Bull Sluice* are solid Class III's. Most boaters attempt to catch the small eddy along the left bank just above the first drop. This close vantage point provides one last chance to reconsider your decision.

To the novice, the route through *Bull Sluice* may look relatively simple, but the safest route can vary with the changing water levels. When the river is low, the rapid may be reduced to a difficult Class IV, but at high levels it rates a sold Class V and may even reach Class VI intensity. The only really safe way to run *Bull Sluice* is on foot, with your boat on your head. Portage over the boulder pile on the Georgia side of the river. There have been numerous fatalities here, and a surpising number have occurred at low water levels as boaters have become entrapped in submerged rocks. To spectators, all rapids look pretty easy, but anyone who has ever run this one will tell you that your impression of *Bull Sluice* changes quickly once you are a few feet from the brink of the drop. Those who have capsized in *Bull Sluice* often compare it to being flushed down a giant toilet (A memory that this writer unfortunately can relate to).

Trails on both sides of the river lead to *Bull Sluice*, and its proximity to the highway usually ensures plenty of spectators. Below the drop, several hundred yards of easy shoals provide an anticlimactic end to the whitewater carnage just experienced. A broad sandy beach just before the bridge provides a nice takeout spot but the steep 0.2 mile carry back to the parking area will surely seem much more difficult after a long day on the river.

Paddlers Encounter *Decapitation Rock* in Bull Sluice

Section III Access Points for Boaters

Earl's Ford: From Clayton, Take US Hwy 76 east for nine miles, crossing into South Carolina over the Chattooga River. Continue 2.1 miles to Chattooga Ridge Road on the left. Turn here and proceed 5.8 miles to the four-way stop sign. Turn left onto Earl's Ford Road and follow it approximately 3.5 miles to the parking area at the end of the road.

Sandy Ford: From the Chattooga Ridge Road / Earl's Ford intersection, proceed 3.0 miles to FS 721A on the left. Follow the winding road 1.6 miles to the parking area at the end of the road.

Fall Creek Trail: From the US Hwy 76 bridge, head east for 2.1 miles and turn onto Chattooga Ridge Road. Proceed 2.1 miles to Fall Creek Road (FS 722) on the left (From Earl's Ford Road, proceed 3.9 miles south). Follow FS 722 to FS 769 on the left and proceed to the parking area at the end of the road.

US Hwy 76: From Clayton, follow US Hwy 76 east for 9 miles to the Forest Service parking area on the South Carolina side of the river.

Paddling Section III - General Information

Gradient:	29 feet per mile
Width:	great variation in width; extremes can run from 10' - 200'
Length:	12.5 miles
Seasons:	year round
Acceptable levels:	Minimum 0.8 feet
	Maximum 3.5 feet

Levels above 2.0 are generally considered to be dangerous. Use discretion. Gauge is located downstream of the US Hwy 76 bridge on the South Carolina bank.

Exploring Section III on Foot

Earl's Ford
Sumter National Forest, Oconee County, SC

Trail length: 0.25 mile one way to river
Difficulty: Easy
Elevation change: Approx. 200 feet
Features: Sandy beach along Chattooga River
USGS Quadrangle Map: Rainy Mountain

Directions: *From the Chattooga River bridge on the Georgia / South Carolina line, follow US Hwy 76 east for 2.1 miles. Turn left onto Chattooga Ridge Road and drive 5.8 miles to the four-way stop sign. Turn left onto Earl's Ford Road and proceed approximately 3.5 miles to the parking area at the end of the road.*

Earl's Ford is known primarily as the major launching point for Section III boaters. Hikers will also find the area around the ford a good area to walk and explore. The old road bed descends from the parking area about one-quarter mile down to the river, ending at a broad sandy beach. Although usually littered with boats early in the morning, this beach is often quiet by afternoon, and makes a great spot to wade or picnic. Directly across the river, Warwoman Creek mingles with the Chattooga, providing plenty of cold water for an invigorating swim.

This area contains several good primitive camping spots. Most of these are located near the shady river bank, and are little more than cleared areas in the underbrush. A well-worn path runs down the South Carolina bank, passing most of these camping spots. Be sure to check current Forest Service guidelines before setting up camp (see chapter 7) anywhere in the corridor. Don't assume that just because someone else has camped in a spot that it's permissible.

Sandy Ford
Sumter National Forest, Oconee County, SC

Trail length: 0.25 mile one way to river
Difficulty: Easy
Elevation change: Approx. 200 feet
Features: Chattooga River scenery
USGS Quadrangle Map: Whetstone

Directions: *From the Chattooga River bridge on the Georgia / South Carolina line, follow US Hwy 76 east for 2.1 miles. Turn left onto Chattooga Ridge Road and drive 5.8 miles to the four-way stop sign. Turn left onto Earl's Ford Road and proceed 3.0 miles to FS 721A on the left. Follow FS 721A for 1.6 miles to the parking area at the end of the road.*

Sandy Ford is a scenic pooled area of the Chattooga located about three miles downriver from Earl's Ford. This popular alternate put-in possesses enough picturesque scenery to make it an area worthy of exploring on foot. The surrounding area offers hiking, camping, fishing and swimming opportunities.

From the FS 721A parking area, a quarter-mile path runs west down to the river. The current here is slow and the river quite wide. Directly across is the namesake sandy beach, which is a popular local swimming hole and party place.

Upstream, the lively lower drops of the Class III *Stairsteps* plunge toward Sandy Ford. Huge jagged slabs of rock line the head of the pool on the South Carolina side, creating a lovely scene. The assortment of boulders in the area creates a nice picnic spot from which to watch the parade of whitewater paddlers pass by during the spring and summer.

Several *primitive* paths run along the river banks from Sandy Ford. To the south, an overgrown trail winds down to the top of the *Narrows*. This walk features a wet crossing of beautiful Whetstone Creek just downstream of a nice, broad waterfall. Once across, the path runs fairly flat through an old camping area before reaching the top of the rapid. The path then becomes very rough and steep in spots as it picks its way down river alongside the fluming drop. Some of the largest rocks along the river can be reached with a bit of effort, though this area is potentially very dangerous. These rocks are steep and slippery, and the current here is very strong!

Another overgrown path runs north from Sandy Ford to *Dick's Creek Ledge*. This highly scenic walk features great views of the *Stairsteps*, *Dick's Creek Ledge* and a pretty good look at Dick's Creek Falls across the river. Though extremely overgrown in certain spots, experienced hikers shouldn't have too much trouble negotiating the half-mile up to the ledge. For a close-up view of the Dick's Creek Falls, access the Dick's Creek Falls Trail from the Georgia side of the river. *Hikers should not attempt to cross the river under any circumstances, as the current is very strong. Deaths due to foot entrapment have occurred on the Chattooga.*

The *Stairsteps* above Sandy Ford

Dick's Creek Falls
Chattahoochee National Forest, Rabun County, GA

Trail length: 0.5 mile one way to falls
Difficulty: Easy
Elevation change: Minimal
Features: Dick's Creek Falls, Dick's Creek Ledge
USGS Quadrangle Map: Whetstone

Directions: *From US Hwy 441 north in Clayton, turn right onto Warwoman Road (next to Days Inn) and proceed 5.7 miles to Sandy Ford Road on the right. Follow for 0.65 mile to a low water bridge over Warwoman Creek. Turn left here and proceed four miles. Park just before the second Dick's Creek ford. The trail to the falls begins to the left.*

Beautiful Dick's Creek Falls slides into the majestic Chattooga River over a smooth 50 foot ledge at the end of an easy half-mile trail. One of the greatest aspects of this easy hike is that it not only features a beautiful waterfall, but plenty of other outstanding scenery as well.

At the second ford on Sandy Ford Road, park and walk east on the north side of Dick's Creek. This path makes for a very pleasant, mostly flat stroll through the forest. At 0.4 mile, the path crosses the Bartram & Chattooga River Trail before continuing several hundred yards downstream to the top of the waterfall.

From the rocks adjacent to the top of the falls, hikers can enjoy a sublime view of a massive rock wall as it extends all the way across the river and forms Class IV *Dick's Creek Ledge*. The waterfall is also known as *"Five Finger Falls"* due to the way the waterfall splits into individual tongues as it races down the rock face.

Hwy 76 Bridge - Bull Sluice
Sumter National Forest, Oconee County, SC
Chattahoochee National Forest, Rabun County, GA

Trail length: Short walk to river and Bull Sluice
Difficulty: Easy
Elevation change: Minimal
Features: Bull Sluice, Chattooga River scenery
USGS Quadrangle Map: Rainy Mountain

Directions: *From Clayton, take US Hwy 76 east for nine miles. Cross the Chattooga bridge and turn left into the US Forest Service parking area.*

The most heavily visited single spot in the Chattooga River corridor is the Information Station and put-in at the US Hwy 76 bridge. This location, also known as Rogue's Ferry, is only ten minutes southeast of Clayton, and provides the most practical spot for interested parties to get a look at the famous river.

Visitors will find several information boards and a number of pit toilets here - everything you need. The boater registration board is located behind the building on the paved path that drops to the river put-in. Here a large, inviting beach just upstream of the 76 bridge welcomes waders and picnickers. The skeletal remains of the old highway bridge still remain suspended above the river. Though now rusted and dilapidated, this one lane bridge bears witness to a time when travel through this rugged area was not an afterthought.

Along the paved path to the river, a side trail turns right and runs up river to a newly constructed boardwalk overlooking giant *Bull Sluice*, one of the river's famous Class V rapids. During the warm summer months this is a great spot to watch scores of boaters negotiate the frenzied whitewater.

Across the river on the Georgia bank a narrow, unmaintained trail forks off the Chattooga River Trail and drops down alongside the river several hundred yards below

Bull Sluice. After hopping across Pole Creek, the trail comes along side the mammoth rock outcrop that forms the *Bull.*

From this side of the river, visitors can enjoy a close-up view of the harrowing rapid. Of particular interest is to look at the faces of paddlers just before they plunge through the drop. Boaters are just a few feet from the rocks on the Georgia side as they spill through the sluice, and great photos can be made from this spot. Use extreme caution here, especially if you have children. The rocks around *Bull Sluice* are very steep and dangerous.

Chattooga River Trail
Chattahoochee National Forest, Rabun County, GA

Trail length: 10 miles
Difficulty: Moderate
Elevation change: Approx. 300 feet
Features: Chattooga River scenery
USGS Quadrangle Map: Rainy Mountain, Whetstone

Directions: *From Clayton, take US Hwy 76 east for nine miles. Cross the Chattooga bridge and turn left into the US Forest Service parking area. See Bartram & Chattooga River Trail information in Chapter 4 for directions to Sandy Ford trailhead.*

This segment of the popular Chattooga River Trail gently winds ten miles north from the US Hwy 76 bridge to its junction with the Bartram Trail just west of Sandy Ford. This long, moderate path closely parallels its namesake for only about two of its total ten mile length, but is usually no more than a quarter-mile from the Chattooga at any given time.

The Hwy 76 trail head originates in the small parking area on the Georgia side of the highway bridge. Look for the boulder with the inscription *"Chattooga River Trail"*. Throughout its entire length, this trail features white diamond-shaped blazes.

The most scenic portion of the trail occurs as the path comes alongside the river. From mile 5.5 to approximately mile 7.0, the trail closely follows the river bank, allowing hikers to explore the many sandy beaches and small shoals found along this section. Although no major rapids occur here, the scenery is outstanding and numerous primitive camping possibilities occur at regular intervals. Though river exposure is minimal, plenty of good hiking is encountered as the trail winds along the many low ridges west of the Chattooga.

The trail crosses Sandy Ford Road at mile point ten, and continues 0.3 mile up to a junction with the Bartram Trail. The path extends north an additional ten miles to Russell Bridge at Hwy 28. Nearby Sandy Ford is quite scenic. Be sure to walk down the road from the trail crossing and explore this picturesque area.

Though this portion of the Chattooga River Trail does not provide the amount of river scenery one might expect, it is nonetheless quite worthy of a visit. The hike usually provides a good deal of isolation, and allows access to some of the river corridor's most pristine scenery.

The CHATTOOGA
Wild and Scenic River

6

Section IV

80 The Chattooga Wild and Scenic River

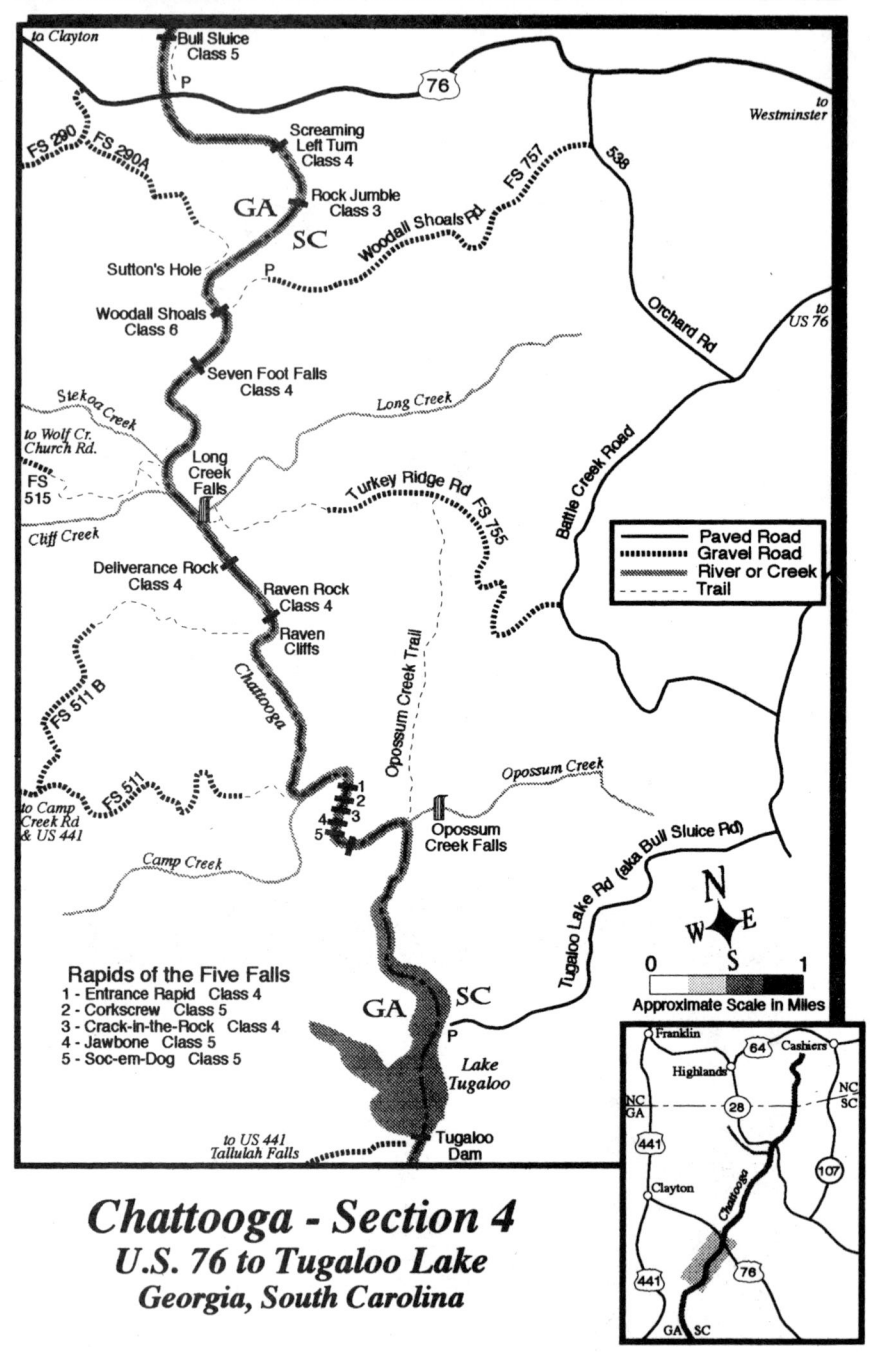

Chattooga - Section 4
U.S. 76 to Tugaloo Lake
Georgia, South Carolina

Section IV

US Hwy 76 to Lake Tugaloo

Ultimate Whitewater and breathtaking scenery.

If thundering southern whitewater is your goal, then Section IV of the Chattooga is as close to heaven as you can come. This mighty seven mile stretch drops an average of 45 feet per mile as it crashes through narrow canyons and over twisting drops down to the its death in the silent backwaters of Lake Tugaloo. Imposing sheer cliffs and splashing waterfalls enhance the wilderness setting, creating a magnificent destination for boaters and hikers alike. Regardless of your method of exploration - by boat or on foot, rugged Section IV will require the best of your outdoor skills.

Floating Section IV
US Hwy 76 Bridge to Woodall Shoals - Mile 0.0 to 2.0

Section IV is known around the world as one of the most beautiful, exciting and challenging whitewater runs anywhere. The seven miles of whitewater below the Hwy 76 bridge is far more difficult than the preceeding sections, and should never be taken lightly, especially when the river is above 2.0'. Boaters must utilize all safety precautions - especially your common sense and good judgement. Carefully reconsider your skill level before attempting Section IV and consider taking a guided rafting trip or accompanying an experienced group before attempting on your own. *Numerous fatalities attest to the danger of this portion of the river - it's reputation is well-deserved!*

The Section IV journey begins at the sandy beach just upstream from the Hwy 76 bridge. From here, several hundred yards of calm water takes you around a bend to the first real fun of the day, an easy Class III known as *Surfing Rapid*. This is a favorite spot for body surfing, and provides those who decide to stay in their boats with a good warm-up rapid.

Some of the real action begins just ahead, as a few hundred yards downstream is *Screaming Left Turn*, a nominal Class IV drop. The current in *SLT* swings boaters sharply around several boulders before funneling all the way back across the river. Enter the rapid near the right bank and work your way across to the left. The current works hard to push you back to the right for the final drop. Like any piece of appreciable whitewater, it's a great ride - provided you stay upright.

Approximately one-half mile below *Screaming Left Turn*, the river appears to be choked by a large series of boulders. This marks the entrance to *Rock Jumble*, an appropriately named Class III. *Rock Jumble* is best negotiated near the left center, although there are numerous possible routes depending on the water level. The *Jumble* can be a bumpy ride, so be prepared to put a few scratches on that new boat.

Downstream the river calms considerably, featuring peaceful scenery and a noteworthy swimming area known as *Sutton's Hole*. Boaters will recognize this area by a relative lack of underbrush and a well-trodden beach. If finding a place for a swim while boating is on your list of priorities, better do it here. From here on down there aren't too many possibilities.

Shortly downstream an immense granite shelf juts into the river from the South Carolina side and an ominous roar alerts boaters to the presence of *Woodall Shoals*, one of the most deceiving and thereby dangerous drops on the entire Chattooga. Take out of the river well above the drop and walk down to **SCOUT** this innocent looking spot. The drop along the South Carolina bank is over a smooth 4 foot ledge into a small pool, but a keen eye will notice that the water below the ledge flows back upstream for some distance, indicating the presence of a strong hydraulic.

Numerous deaths here over the years make a strong case for portaging around this drop. If the river is running above 2.0' there is a steep but rocky sneak route along the right bank. The

Forest Service has designated *Woodall Shoals* as a Class VI due to the dangerous hydraulic. Otherwise, the rapid would rate as Class III. Plenty of additional strong shoals rush below the initial drop, leading to a large recovery pool and beach on the South Carolina side. If the trip so far has pushed your boating skills to the limit, better exit here. A short, steep hike on the Carolina side leads up to a parking area along FS 757 (Woodall Shoals Road). Better to exit the river here than take any chances in the powerful whitewater downstream.

Floating Section IV
Woodall Shoals to Lake Tugaloo - Mile 2.0 to 7.0

Below *Woodall Shoals*, the character of the river begins to change drastically. The previously wide riverbed narrows considerably as powerful currents push violently between huge boulders and sheer rock walls, and the difficulty of the drops increase accordingly.

In the initial half-mile below *Woodall*, several lively Class III chutes with good waves are encountered. As the river continues to narrow, it enters a rugged gorge lined with steep rock walls and smooth boulders. When a distinct horizon line can be seen, beach *quickly* on the right. This is the brink of Class IV *Seven Foot Falls*, one of this section's most dramatic drops.

This heart-stopping ledge is actually composed of two tongues of water compressed into one waterfall. The right tongue shoots out over the left, and the combined current then slams headlong into the gorge wall just a stone's throw away. Boaters often disappear into the highly aerated water at the base and pop-up a split second before slamming into rocks along the left bank. A quick recovery at the base can prevent this unique experience. Above 1.6', a rocky chute appears along the right bank that can be run, though it is quite rough.

Take full advantage of the next two miles, as it offers a break of moderate whitewater and superlative scenery. Just over a half-mile below *Seven Foot Falls* in a broad left bend in the river, scenic Stekoa Creek enters from the Georgia side. Look up into the creek gorge and you can glimpse several small falls and shoals. Unfortunately, the water entering the Chattooga via Stekoa Creek is often stained with unsightly sediment. During periods of high water the creek also can carry dangerous coliform bacteria. Stekoa Creek provides the major drainage for the Clayton-Mountain City area, and efforts are continuing to improve the quality of runoff, something you may be thankful for if you take a spill downstream.

Stekoa Creek also signals the beginning of a long series of lively Class III shoals. There are many possible routes through this series of whitewater, but generally they are negotiated near the left bank.

Just below these drops stay left and look for a creek entering the river. Pull ashore just upstream of the confluence and magnificent Long Creek Falls comes into view. For years a favorite lunch spot, this inviting 30 foot waterfall spills over a broken rock face just a few hundred feet inland from the Chattooga. Long Creek then flows over several small ledges before merging into the river. Boaters can often be found sunning on the rocks or even taking an invigorating shower in the spray from the falls. One word of caution: *the rocks around the waterfall are very slippery! Do not climb the waterfall!*

Long Creek Falls

Further down river a giant boulder appears to block the river channel. Named "*Deliverance Rock*" due to its appearance in several of the movie's scenes, this Class III-IV drop should be run to the left of the giant boulder. The current here is strong, and fluctuating water levels may alter the best course. Once *Deliverance Rock* has been negotiated, your attention will be drawn to a towering rock escarpment known as Raven Rock Cliffs, looming several hundred yards downstream.

Raven Rock Cliffs

A few hundred feet upstream of the cliffs, the Chattooga roars over a six foot high river-wide Class IV ledge called *Raven's Chute*. Though most of the river spills directly over the sheer drop, a convenient tongue of water slides diagonally down the ledge against the left bank, pushing boaters back to the right and into a nice recovery pool. At higher water levels a nice hole develops at the base of the tongue. Though some advanced boaters run the sheer drops along the ledge at high water levels, this is not advisable due to the presence of a number of large boulders at the base.

The next mile is eerily conspicuous for its lack of significant whitewater, and is aptly called *"The Calm Before the Storm"*. Take advantage of this peaceful stretch, for it allows boaters one last opportunity to relax before encountering the grand climax just ahead. Keep a sharp eye out for several small sandy beaches on the right preceding Camp Creek. A short trail leads from here up to FS 511 (Water Gauge Road), the last good exit point before reaching *Five Falls*. Around the bend below

Camp Creek is a sight that may make you wish you were back tubing along the river's placid Section II.

The Canyon of the Five Falls

Five Falls provides the most appropriate crescendo to a whitewater run found anywhere, and is primarily responsible for the nasty reputation the Chattooga enjoys. Here in a 400 yard long gorge, the Chattooga plunges in an absolute frenzy over five back-to-back rapids, descending approximately 75 feet. Scouting and portaging are difficult and strenuous, as the gorge walls are littered with mammoth boulders and sheer rock faces. The currents are strong and tricky, and any recovery pools are very small. This is a dangerous area, and deserves a boater's complete attention. *Numerous drownings have occurred here over the years.*

Boulder-strewn Five Falls

The *Five Falls* challenge kicks off with the colorfully named *Entrance Rapid* (aka *First Falls*). This long, complex Class IV begins on the left side of the river, works through a lengthy boulder garden over several small drops, then pushes into an eddy at the brink of a wide, rocky ledge. Paddlers must peel out of the

Corkscrew - Class V

eddy and drop to the right of a large boulder at the base of the ledge. Throw ropes must be set below the rapid, as just downstream is something you wouldn't want to swim through.

Corkscrew, as the name implies, is a twisting, churning, exploding flume of powerful aerated water complete with big waves and unpredictable holes. This solid Class V is famous for its ability to flip boats, and is generally regarded as one of the wildest rapids on the river. *Corkscrew* can be scouted from either side, but portaging is easier along the right bank. Throw ropes should be set up below the rapid, as the current pushes wildly into the left bank, then directly into the deceptively dangerous *Crack-in-the-Rock* below.

Class IV *Crack-in-the-Rock*, the tamest-looking of the *Five Falls*, cannot be taken lightly. Here, the river drops over a five foot high river-wide ledge through three distinct openings, or cracks. The right crack is by far the widest, and is the recommended route. Middle crack can be run when the river is low, but is only about 3 feet wide and is not recommended. *Avoid left crack at all costs.* Numerous accidents and several deaths have occurred here. There is a sizable pool beneath the rapid, but the current here is quite strong, and pushes directly into the

Jawbone - Class IV-V

next two rapids. Boaters who capsize must be rescued immediately.

Next up is impressive *Jawbone*, a big-water Class IV-V. *Jawbone* resembles a giant funnel as water pours into the center of this drop from three sides. Paddlers should enter from the right side and attempt to run down the center. A small eddy on the upper left edge can sometimes be caught in order to provide another vantage point before committing to the rapid. From the eddy, run down the surging current through powerful waves and head to the left of the large rock at the base of the rapid in the center of the river. This is *"Hydroelectric Rock"*, and is nearly completely undercut. Over the years, harrowing tales have been told by paddlers as both boats and people have been sucked underneath and through to the downstream side of the rock. Again, set throw ropes below the rapid, as yet another violent drop is just downstream. Scout *Jawbone* from either bank before running.

Immediately below *Jawbone* is the infamous *Sock-em-Dog*, a solid Class V at any water level, and a dangerous Class V-VI at high water. *Sock-em-Dog* is a seven foot vertical drop compounded by the presence of twin hydraulics at the base. The current pushes hard to the left of the main drop, positioned just off the right bank. Most boaters head for the "hump" of water at the brink of the drop. Nicknamed the *"launching pad"*, some boats seem to become airborne for a split second before smashing into the violent hole at the base. Boaters should get up as much forward speed as possible, as this hole is quite grabby. Numerous rocks scattered about the base can do a great deal of damage to boats, so plan your route carefully. While *Sock-em-Dog* is dangerous at any water level, it becomes much more difficult and dangerous above 1.6'. Scouting is best accomplished from the right bank. Portage the drop over the rocks on the left bank.

Below *Sock-em-Dog* is another cheerfully named river feature - *"Dead Man's Pool"*, which provides quite an abrupt contrast to the whitewater carnage above. This huge pool usually contains quite a collection of debris - logs, limbs, styrofoam, shoes - anything washed downstream.

Only one more named rapid remains - *Shoulder Bone*. This easy Class III lies just below *"Dead Man's Pool"* and is run just to the left of a large overhanging rock. Downstream a small beach on the left allows boaters to experience *"Ambush Rock,"*

Sock-em-Dog "Anybody seen my canoe?"

a favorite point for taking a plunge into the river. Long a popular stopping point for commercial outfitters, *Ambush Rock* provides a great spot to picnic or rest. Due to the dangers involved in jumping into any body of water, resist the urge to use *Ambush Rock* as a diving platform - you never know what the current has washed downstream.

The confluence of Opossum Creek from the left signals the last few hundred yards of freedom for the Chattooga, as the river soon gives up its *Wild and Scenic* designation and becomes silent Lake Tugaloo. A painfully slow two mile paddle is required to reach the take-out on the South Carolina side at Bull Sluice Road / Tugaloo Lake Road. Those who experience Section IV via commercial outfitters may be lucky enough to have a power boat pull you to the ramp. Either way, enjoy the beauty of this undeveloped lake and take the opportunity to reflect upon the thrills and beauty of the Chattooga River.

Major Section IV Access Points

US Hwy 76 Bridge: *Located nine miles southeast of Clayton on US Hwy 76. Parking area and boat ramp are located on the South Carolina side of the river.*

Woodall Shoals: *Proceed east from the US Hwy 76 bridge for 2.5 miles. Turn right onto Orchard Road and proceed 0.4 mile to Woodall Shoals Road (FS 757). Follow the gravel road for several miles to the parking area at the end of the road.*

Lake Tugaloo: *Follow directions above, and proceed past Woodall Shoals Road for an additional two miles to a stop sign. Turn right onto Battle Creek Road and proceed 2.5 miles, then veer right onto Damascus Church Road. Proceed 1.2 miles to Bull Sluice Road (PU 5) on the right. Follow the winding, sometimes steep road 3.5 miles to the parking area alongside the lake.*

Paddling Section IV - General Information

Gradient:	45 feet per mile
Width:	great variation in width; extremes can run from 10' - 200'
Length:	9 miles from US 76 to Tugaloo Lake Road on SC side
	10 miles to Tugaloo Dam on GA side
Seasons:	year round
Acceptable levels:	Minimum 0.8 feet
	Maximum 2.5 feet (open boat)
	Maximum 4.0 feet (decked boat with expert paddler)

Levels above 2.0 are generally considered to be very dangerous. Use discretion. Gauge is located downstream of the US Hwy 76 bridge on the South Carolina bank.

Crack-in-the-Rock

Exploring Section IV on Foot

Sutton's Hole
Chattahoochee National Forest, Rabun County, Georgia

Trail length: 0.3 to 0.6 mile one way
Difficulty: Easy
Elevation change: Approx. 300 feet
Features: Swimming hole along Chattooga River
USGS Quadrangle Map: Rainy Mountain

Directions: *From the Chattooga River bridge on the Georgia / South Carolina line, follow US Hwy 76 west for approximately 0.7 mile to FS 290 on the left. Follow FS 290 for 0.3 mile to its junction with FS 290A on the left. FS 290A is very bumpy and rutted - best to park here and walk 0.3 mile to its dead end, then pick up the trail (look for the marker on the right side of the clearing at the end of 290A) which winds another 0.3 mile down to the river.*

Sutton's Hole Trail makes an easy 0.3 mile descent to the river's edge following an old logging road. The path is quite broad, but often rocky and steep, terminating along the Chattooga at a spot known locally as *Sutton's Hole*. Long a favorite swimming hole for both paddlers and hikers, this natural beach lies nestled along one of the few placid stretches of Section IV. The scenery isn't grand by Section IV standards, but this is a nice spot to sun, swim and just relax. A normally overgrown path runs downstream for several hundred yards toward beautiful *Woodall Shoals*, but requires a potentially dangerous river crossing in order to reach the heavily visited South Carolina side.

Woodall Shoals
Sumter National Forest, Oconee County, South Carolina

Trail length: 0.25 mile one way
Difficulty: Easy
Elevation change: Approx. 150 feet
Features: Whitewater, rock formations, scenic beauty
USGS Quadrangle Map: Rainy Mountain

Directions: *From the Chattooga River bridge on the Georgia / South Carolina line, follow US Hwy 76 east for 2.5 miles. Turn right onto Orchard Road and proceed 0.4 mile to Woodall Shoals Road (FS 757) on the right. Follow the gravel road for 2 miles to the parking area at the end of the road.*

One of the Chattooga's most beautiful areas to visit on foot is *Woodall Shoals*. Here the river crashes over a mammoth granite shelf in a fury of roaring whitewater. This scenic area is quite easy to access and therefore remains one of the Chattooga River's most popular destinations.

Two separate quarter-mile paths descend to the river, each beginning on opposite sides of the parking area. Both trails end at the same spot close to the edge of a huge pool bordered by an inviting sandy beach. Beyond the pool to the right, an enormous granite shelf diverts the river into the shoals. At normal water levels, only a small picturesque series of cascades spill from the main river to fill the pool. From this vantage point, though the river isn't visible, the unmistakable sounds and smells attest to its close proximity.

A short scramble up the granite ledge to the right of the pool brings visitors to the top of the shoals. Upstream, the river is somewhat placid, with only a few scattered shoals extending upstream to *Sutton's Hole*. If the river is very low (below 0.6') this area becomes a popular swimming spot, with swimmers and sunbathers littering the rocks. Even at low water levels, stay well above the initial drop and its infamous "keeper" hydraulic, the site of numerous drownings over the years. This ledge looks innocent enough, but the Forest Service has designated this drop as a Class VI - the most difficult rating attainable. Use extreme caution - a swim here could be your last!

Below this initial drop, *Woodall* offers up another 50 yards of exciting Class III whitewater. At the base of the shoals, a large pool nestles against a broad rocky beach on the South Carolina bank. This is perhaps the best spot on the river for rock-skipping, and is also a great spot to watch boaters running the lower sections of *Woodall Shoals*.

There are several camping sites scattered about this scenic area. Several of these border the parking area, and others can be reached via the path that winds down to the shoals from the northwest corner of the parking area. Please observe the *"No Camping"* signs posted down along the river, though the temptation has always been great. This area is both beautiful and fragile, and visitors should be very careful to avoid adversely impacting the environment.

Path to Seven Foot Falls
Sumter National Forest, Oconee County, South Carolina

Trail length: Approx. 0.5 mile one way
Difficulty: Moderate to Difficult
Elevation change: Minimal
Features: Whitewater, rock formations, scenic beauty
USGS Quadrangle Map: Rainy Mountain

Directions: *Follow directions to Woodall Shoals. Descend from the parking area to the rocky beach below the shoals. Step across the small stream and follow the primitive path downstream.*

Though definitely not a *maintained* footpath, there is a rough primitive trail that runs along the South Carolina bank from *Woodall Shoals* down to *Seven Foot Falls*.

Even though *Seven Foot Falls* is easier to reach in the cool months of the year, the thick undergrowth of spring and summer shouldn't deter anyone bent on visiting this splendidly wild location.

About 0.3 mile below *Woodall Shoals*, the path begins to climb over several house-sized boulders. Be careful here, as some of these rocks rise 20 feet above the narrowing Chattooga. When the river bends sharply left and seems to disappear into a large boulder pile, you have arrived at the brink of the falls.

Seven Foot Falls is really a combination of two chutes squeezed together into one waterfall. One tongue shoots out over the other, creating a drop that can easily flip paddlers. The mammoth boulders surrounding the pool can be dangerous and intimidating, yet they offer the non-paddler a ringside seat to the action. One particular slab places spectators within about 10 feet of boaters as they take the plunge over this powerful Class IV rapid. Note: this area is dangerous and not suitable for children.

Cliff Creek & Stekoa Creek
Chattahoochee National Forest, Rabun County, Georgia

Trail length: Approx. 1.5 miles of old logging roads
Difficulty: Moderate
Elevation change: Approx. 400 feet
Features: Stekoa Creek, Cliff Creek, Chattooga vistas
USGS Quadrangle: Rainy Mountain

Directions: *From the intersection of US Hwy 441 and US Hwy 76 in Clayton, head south on Hwy 441 for 7.3 miles. Turn left onto Wolf Creek Rd. and proceed 3.6 miles to Wolf Creek Church Rd. on the right. Follow Wolf Creek Church Rd. for 0.6 mile. At the church, the road becomes FS 515. Continue straight ahead for 2.1 miles to a large parking area where the road becomes much more primitive.*

Even though there are no maintained trails leading to the river in this area, a network of old logging roads provides access to this seldom visited part of the Chattooga. Two beautiful mountain streams flow into the river here, each offering a variety of excellent scenery.

For visitors who are able to read and follow a topo map, this area is quite interesting. An old logging road runs from the end of FS 515 down to within sight of Cliff Creek. Eventually the road ascends through a low gap before terminating high above the Stekoa Creek gorge. A short but steep walk down the trail from the road's end will deposit hikers along the Chattooga river bank just a stone's throw from the picturesque confluence of Stekoa Creek with the river. From the river bank, *Deliverance Rock* and *Raven Cliffs* can be seen far downstream.

Stekoa Creek enters the Chattooga

From the low gap preceding the end of the logging road, another overgrown roadbed descends southeast to the confluence of Cliff Creek with the river. Once off the logging roads, this is real back country hiking. *Be sure you have a topo map and compass before you visit.* This area is quite overgrown and it is very easy for visitors to get turned around here.

Long Creek Falls
Chattahoochee National Forest, Rabun County, Georgia

Trail length: 2.0 miles one way from main parking area
Difficulty: Moderate
Elevation change: Approx. 400 feet
Features: Long Creek Falls, Chattooga River
USGS Quadrangle: Rainy Mountain

Directions: *From the Chattooga River bridge on the Georgia / South Carolina line, follow US 76 east for 2.5 miles. Turn right onto Orchard Road and follow 2.4 miles to the stop sign. Turn right onto Battle Creek Road and proceed 1.4 miles to Turkey Ridge Road (FS 755) on the right. Follow FS 755 for 2.9 miles to the large gravel parking area or proceed another one mile along the rough, unmaintained jeep road to its deadend. The trail begins here beyond the vehicle-blocking mounds.*

Magnificent Long Creek Falls is perhaps the most beautiful of the Chattooga's tributary waterfalls. Located several hundred feet inland from the river, Long Creek Falls plunges over a broken 30 foot ledge in two distinct tongues before rushing over several small shoals down to the Chattooga. A well-worn path climbs up the left side of the creek to provide a close-up view. Many visitors have been known to step beneath the plunge for an invigorating shower, but exercise great caution, as the rocks here are very slippery! *By all means, do not attempt to climb the falls!*

From the main parking area 2.9 miles from Battle Creek Road, continue down the jeep road for an additional mile. Here the road ends, but the trail continues along the roadbed beyond several vehicle-blocking mounds of dirt. Follow the trail west for approximately 0.5 mile. At this point the trail turns sharply northward, paralleling the nearby river. The path then becomes somewhat more overgrown. Keep a sharp eye out for a side path on the left which cuts down the steep mountain side about

0.4 mile beyond the bend to the north. The sound of splashing water should alert you to this path's proximity. Look for surveyors tape which is often hanging on a low limb. The path drops rapidly, eventually entering a thick grove of laurel and rhododendron before emerging alongside the Chattooga just a few yards downstream of the Long Creek confluence. In order to negotiate the path that approaches the base of the falls, hikers must wade across the normally shallow creek.

This hike usually provides a good degree of solitude, although the falls can become a bit crowded during the warmer months, especially if a rafting outfitter is paying a visit.

Raven Cliffs Trail
Chattahoochee National Forest, Rabun County, Georgia

Trail length: 1.6 miles one way from FS 511-511B junction
Difficulty: Moderate
Elevation change: Approx. 600 feet
Features: Raven Cliffs, Raven's Chute
USGS Quadrangle Map: Rainy Mountain

Directions: *From the intersection of US Hwy 76 & US Hwy 441 in Clayton, take Hwy 441 south for 8.3 miles and turn left onto Camp Creek Road. Proceed 1.3 miles and turn left onto FS 511 (Water Gauge Road). Follow the one-lane gravel road for 2.5 miles to FS 511B on the left. Park here. If you have a good 4WD vehicle, you may choose to follow the very bumpy and rutted road for approximately 0.8 mile to its end.*

Raven Cliffs is one of the most scenic non-whitewater features on the lower Chattooga. This 200 foot escarpment rises ominously above the river just downstream from Class IV *Raven's Chute*. A nice 0.8 mile path winds down to the river just across from the cliffs, providing impressive views of both attractions.

An old roadbed leaves the clearing at the east end of FS

511B, descending gently through a mixed hardwood forest for 0.6 mile. Old white diamond-shaped blazes mark this path. Beyond the 0.6 mile point, the path descends sharply into the rugged gorge through a series of prolonged switchbacks. At the base of the slope alongside the river is a large *unofficial* primitive camping area nestled beneath shady hemlocks and pines. Numerous old fire rings attest to the popularity of this spot.

Raven's Chute - Class IV

About 25 yards distant, the mighty Chattooga surges through the rock-strewn gorge beneath the rocky facade of rugged *Raven Cliffs*. A short 100+ yard rock-hop upstream provides good views of *Raven's Chute*. If your timing is good you may be treated to some entertaining whitewater antics as watercraft of all types negotiate the slide across the river against the South Carolina bank. Hikers who climb the large ledge that forms the rapid can gaze far upstream and view imposing *Deliverance Rock*.

Opossum Creek Trail
Sumter National Forest, Oconee County, SC

Trail length: 2 miles one way to river
Difficulty: Moderate to river; Difficult to Five Falls
Elevation change: Approx. 800 feet
Features: Opossum Creek Falls, Canyon of the Five Falls
USGS Quadrangle Map: Rainy Mountain

Directions: *From the Chattooga River bridge on the Georgia / South Carolina line, follow US 76 east for 2.5 miles. Turn right onto Orchard Road and follow 2.4 miles to the stop sign. Turn right onto Battle Creek Road and proceed 1.4 miles to Turkey Ridge Road (FS 755) on the right. Follow FS 755 for 2.2 miles and park on the left where FS 755F intersects the main road. The trail begins about 75 yards back down the road and is marked by a metal trail sign.*

Rebuilt following a destructive tornado in the spring of 1994, the Opossum Creek Trail was moved slightly west of its original route. The newly developed and highly improved trail follows delightful Camp Branch for most of its noisy journey down to the river and terminates in the sandy floodplain along the Chattooga's east bank.

Once at the river there are numerous points of interest to explore. The trail's namesake - Opossum Creek, enters the river just a stone's throw downstream. The original trail runs back upstream along Opossum Creek for approximately 0.25 mile to beautiful Opossum Creek Falls, a real sleeper among local waterfalls. Opossum Creek Falls tumbles over a steep cliff, plunging wildly over two major drops for a total descent exceeding 100 feet. The beauty and power of this waterfall usually surprises first-time visitors.

A rugged, primitive path runs up river from the Opossum Creek confluence to the *Canyon of the Five Falls*, the Chattooga's most infamous stretch of whitewater. *Rugged* and *primitive* are the key words here, as this quarter mile trek requires bushwhacking and rock-hopping along the river's edge, or scrambling up steep, slippery mountain slopes. If the river is high, you may have to get wet or else do some climbing. *The best advice here is to not even attempt to reach Five Falls on foot unless you are in extremely good shape and not afraid of scrambling over steep rocks.* Any type of accident here could have fatal results, so know your skill level and use all safety precautions.

Opossum Creek Falls

For those who accept the risks, *Five Falls* is a most worthy destination. Here the Chattooga roars through a boulder-strewn quarter-mile long gorge over five back-to-back rapids, culminating in a plunge through the Class V frenzy known as *Sock-em-Dog*. Heading upstream, hikers will then pass *Jawbone* (V), *Crack-in-the-Rock* (IV), *Corkscrew* (V), and finally come to *Entrance Rapid* (IV). There is no real trail leading upstream, but the bare rocks can be negotiated.

The canyon's huge boulders and mammoth rock slabs provide a great place to watch the parade of boaters as they challenge the powerful whitewater. In the cold months visitors may even have the canyon all to themselves - a real treat! For all its thrills, this is a potentially dangerous area. Again, any fall here, either onto the rocks or into the river, could prove fatal. *This is not a hike for children*, but for those in good shape who are used to strenuous hiking, *Five Falls* is a magnificent destination!

Camp Creek Access
Chattahoochee National Forest, Rabun County, Georgia

Trail length: 0.25 mile to river; 0.5 mile to Five Falls
Difficulty: Moderate to river; Difficult to Five Falls
Elevation change: Approx. 200 feet
Features: Canyon of the Five Falls
USGS Quadrangle Map: Rainy Mountain

Directions: *From the intersection of US Hwy 76 & US Hwy 441 in Clayton, take Hwy 441 south for 8.3 miles and turn left onto Camp Creek Road. Proceed 1.3 miles and turn left onto FS 511 (Water Gauge Road). Follow the one-lane gravel road for 4 bumpy miles to its end.*

An easy 0.25 mile path winds down to the river along the Georgia side several hundred yards upstream of the *Five Falls* area. This trail runs alongside a peaceful stretch of the Chattooga aptly nicknamed *"The Calm Before the Storm"*. The path runs downstream past several sandy beaches and through numerous old camping sites before terminating at the river's confluence with scenic Camp Creek.

The infamous *Five Falls* section lies only about 0.25 mile downstream, but reaching it can present quite a frustrating challenge. To follow the river downstream will require scrambling over rocks, climbing over and through logs and debris, and perhaps even some wading if the river is low. Hikers may even be forced to scramble up the steep mountainside to climb through the underbrush. If you choose to attempt this route, be aware that it won't be easy - there is no real trail.

Those determined enough to tolerate all this hard work will be rewarded with an awesome view of the canyon, as the Chattooga drops out of sight over five back-to-back rapids. If you choose to venture downstream, *be aware that the area is steep and the rocks very slippery! The current here is tremendous, and anyone falling into the river would have little hope of getting out unaided.*

Another possible way to access *Five Falls* from the Georgia side involves locating the old logging road that roughly follows Camp Creek upstream (south) from the river. This road is located just west of the creek, and is usually within several hundred feet of the stream. Follow the roadbed for approximately 0.25 mile. Look to the left and locate the point where the road fords Camp Creek. Once across, follow a path east, ascending several hundred yards into a gap. From here, follow the overgrown roadbed to the left for several hundred yards. Find a spot lacking in undergrowth and descend down the steep slopes (to the east) through the relatively open forest. With luck, you'll emerge from the woods at the lower end of *Five Falls* just downstream of Class V *Sock-em-Dog*.

Either of these two routes involve rugged hiking through dense undergrowth and along unmarked and unmaintained paths. If you decide to visit *Five Falls* from the Georgia side, *be sure to take a topographical map and a compass.* You may need them.

Five Falls Whitewater - Section IV

The CHATTOOGA
Wild and Scenic River

7

Rules & Regulations
Facts & Figures

A paddler disappears into Section IV's rugged Jawbone.

Forest Service Regulations
Chattooga River Corridor

- Each float party leader must register.
- All floaters on Sections III & IV must wear a life jacket rated *"Coast Guard Approved"*. On Sections I & II, boaters must have a life saving device with them.
- All persons in decked craft, and ALL floaters below Woodall Shoals, must wear a helmet.
- Minimum party size:
  Above Earl's Ford - 2 persons, 1 craft
  Below Earl's Ford - 2 persons, 2 craft
- Inner tubes are prohibited below Earl's Ford.
- Rafts must have a minimum of 2 air chambers.
- All floating is prohibited above State Hwy 28.
- Air mattresses, motorized craft, or other craft deemed unsuitable by the US Forest Service are prohibited.
- Motorized vehicles are prohibited on all closed roads. (Contact Forest Service offices for possible amendments concerning ATV use).
- All commercial trips must be under a special permit issued by the Forest Service at Mtn. Rest, SC.
- Camping is permitted at any location in the corridor, not closed by signs, that is more than 0.25 mile from a road, and at least 50 feet from a trail, stream, or the river.

Local Forest Service Offices

- Sumter National Forest /Andrew Pickens Ranger District
  112 Andrew Pickens Circle, Mountain Rest, SC 29664
  (864) 638-9568
- Nantahala National Forest / Highlands Ranger District
  Route 1, Box 247, Flat Mtn. Rd., Highlands, NC 28741
  (704) 526-3765
- Chattahoochee National Forest / Tallulah Ranger District
  809 US Hwy 441, Clayton, GA 30525
  (706) 782-3320

Whitewater Classifications

- **Class I**   *EASY* - slow current, clear passage.
- **Class II**   *EASY* - moderate current, low ledges, sharp turns, clear passage.
- **Class III** *MEDIUM* - waves numerous or irregular, narrow passages requiring expertise, usually requires scouting.
- **Class IV**   *DIFFICULT* - long rapids with powerful or irregular waves, rocks, eddies; requires precise maneuvering, mandatory scouting.
- **Class V**   *VERY DIFFICULT* - long, turbulent rapids, heavy obstructions, violent currents, big drops, mandatory scouting.
- **Class VI**   *EXTRAORDINARILY DIFFICULT* - limit of navigability, danger of loss of life, for experts only.

Local Emergency Numbers

- **Rabun County, GA**
  Sheriff - 911 or (706) 782-3612
  Rabun County Rescue - 911 or (706) 782-3333 or 782-7777
  Rabun County Memorial Hospital
    South Main St., Clayton (706) 782-4233
- **Macon County, NC**
  Sheriff - 911
  Macon County Rescue - 911
  Highlands-Cashiers Hospital
    Hwy 64 E. @ Hospital Dr, Highlands (704) 526-1200
- **Jackson County, NC**
  Sheriff - 911 or (704) 743-3333
  Jackson County Ambulance - 911
  Glenville-Cashiers Rescue - 911 or (704) 586-1911
- **Oconee County, SC**
  Sheriff - 911 or (864) 638-3678
  Rescue & Ambulance - 911

Average Floating Times (hrs)

West Fork to Main River

Water Level	0.5'	1.0'	2.0'
Inner tube	4	3	2
Raft	3	2	1
Canoe	2	1.5	1

Section II - Hwy 28 to Earl's Ford

Water Level	0.5'	1.0'	2.0'
Inner tube	8	6	5
Raft	5	4	3
Canoe/Kayak	4	3	2

Section III - Earl's Ford to US Hwy 76

Water Level	1.0'	2.0'	3.0'
Raft	8	6	5
Canoe	7	5	4
Kayak	6	4	3

Section IV - US Hwy 76 to Woodall Shoals

Water Level	1.0'	2.0'	2.5'
Raft	1.5	1	.75
Canoe	1.0	.75	.5
Kayak	.75	.5	.5

Section IV - Woodall Shoals to Lake Tugaloo

Water Level	1.0'	2.0'	2.5'
Raft	6.5	6	6
Canoe	6	5	4.5
Kayak	5	4.5	3.5

Water levels for the West Fork and Section II may be obtained at the Russell Bridge gauge. Levels for Sections III & IV may be obtained at the US Hwy 76 gauge located just downstream from the bridge along the South Carolina bank.

Chattooga River Outfitters

- **Nantahala Outdoor Center
  Chattooga River Outpost**
  851A Chattooga Ridge Rd.
  Mountain Rest, SC 29664
  (864) 647-9014 Reservations: (800) 232-RAFT (7238)
  guided whitewater trips

- **Southeastern Expeditions
  Chattooga River Outpost**
  Rt 3 - Box 3178 E
  Clayton, GA 30525
  (706) 782-4331 Reservations: (800) 868-RAFT (7238)
  guided whitewater trips

- **Wildwater, Ltd.
  Chattooga River Outpost**
  PO Box 309
  Long Creek, SC 29658
  (864) 647-9587 Reservations: (800) 451-9972
  guided whitewater trips

- **Chattooga River Adventures**
  14546-B Long Creek Hwy.
  Mountain Rest, SC 29664
  (864)-647-0365
  equipment sales, clinics, rentals, tours, lodging

- **Chattooga Whitewater Shop**
  14239 Long Creek Hwy
  Long Creek, SC 29658
  (864) 647-9083   fax (864) 647-4459
  equipment sales, clinics, rentals

- **Chattooga Rent-A-Raft**
  Hwy 76 East, across from Southeastern Exp.
  (706) 782-1221
  rentals

Chattooga Floating Use

Chattooga Usage Figures 1967 - 1983

Year	Total Use	Private Use	Commercial Use	Average Water Level
1967	100	100	-	-
1968	100	100	-	-
1969	300	300	-	-
1970	800	800	-	-
1971	800	800	-	-
1972[1]	7,600	7,600	-	1.6'
1973	21,000	14,196	6,904	2.1'
1974[2]	28,800	22,274	6,326	1.8'
1975[3]	20,414	13,425	6,989	1.8'
1976	17,100	6,867	10,233	1.9'
1977	17,400	4,311	13,089	1.8'
1978	30,000	10,000	20,000	1.4'
1979	33,600	14,200	19,400	2.0'
1980	43,223	13,961	29,262	1.7'
1981	37,450	11,288	26,162	1.0'
1982	55,129	17,250	37,879	1.5'
1983	53,900	15,430	38,470	1.7'

[1] Movie *Deliverance* filmed on Chattooga River.
[2] May 10 - River designated *Wild and Scenic* by Congress.
[3] First year of commercial permits; first year of private registration and accurate counting;

Chattooga Usage Figures 1984 - 1995*

Year	Total Use	Private Use	Commercial Use	Average Water Level
1984	56,978	17,260	39,718	1.7'
1985	53,742	14,840	38,902	1.2'
1986	39,010	9,450	29,560	.95'
1987	56,790	14,590	42,200	1.3'
1988	49,200	10,900	38,300	1.0'
1989	68,210	18,360	49,850	1.8'
1990	65,806	15,658	50,148	1.4'
1991	71,293	18,738	52,555	1.9'
1992	73,094	20,022	53,072	1.8'
1993	63,051	15,428	47,623	1.4'
1994	82,871	24,590	58,281	1.9'
1995	89,233	27,014	62,219	1.6'

* Commercial figures include raft/clinic clients, guides, and instructors. Includes short-term commercial clinic use after 1990. Includes photographers after 1988. All usage figures courtesy of the U.S. Forest Service, Walhalla, SC.

Adopt-the-Chattooga

The *Adopt-the-Chattooga* program was established in 1990 in order to maintain a clean, healthy river environment. Participating groups agree to pick up trash on an assigned section of the river. Currently over fifteen clubs or organizations are members of the Adopt-the-Chattooga program. Contact the Andrew Pickens Ranger District office of the U.S. Forest Service in Walhalla, S.C. at (864) 638-9568 for details.

Chattooga River Trails

The Chattooga Headwaters

Name	Length	difficulty	main attraction
Whiteside Mtn. Trail	2.0 mile loop	moderate	spectacular views
Sliding Rock	0.1 mile	easy	Cashiers sliding rock
Bullpen bridge	2.0 mile loop	easy	Chattooga gorge
Chattooga Cliffs	2.9 mile loop	moderate	Chattooga Cliffs
Bad Creek Trail	3.5 miles	moderate	Ellicott Rock, river
Ellicott Rock Trail	3.5 miles	moderate	Ellicott Rock, river
Sloan Bridge Trail	7.5 miles	moderate	Ellicott Rock, river
East Fork Trail	2.5 miles	moderate	East Fork Chattooga
Fish hatchery	short walk	easy	fish hatchery, picnic area
King Creek Falls	0.6 mile	easy	beautiful waterfall
Foothills Trail *Sloan Br. to Spoon Auger Falls*	7.3 miles	moderate	scenic views
Chattooga River Trail *Ellicott Rock to Russell Bridge*	14.5 miles	moderate	Chattooga River

Section 1 - The West Fork

Name	Length	difficulty	main attraction
Three Forks Trail			
to Holcomb Cr Falls	1.25 miles	moderate	waterfall
to Three Forks	1.5 miles	difficult	highly scenic gorge
to West Fork	1.5 miles	difficult	West Fork Chattooga
Holcomb Creek Trail	0.6 mile	moderate	beautiful waterfalls

Trail lengths listed are one-way to destination unless otherwise noted.

Chattooga River - Section II

Name	Length	difficulty	main attraction
Bartram & Chattooga River Trail - *Russell Bridge to Sandy Ford*	9.8 miles	moderate	Chattooga scenery

Chattooga River - Section III

Name	Length	difficulty	main attraction
Chattooga River Trail *Sandy Ford to Hwy 76*	10 miles	moderate	Chattooga scenery
Earl's Ford	0.25 mile	easy	Chattooga River
Sandy Ford	0.25 mile	easy	Chattooga River
Dick's Creek Falls	0.5 mile	easy	waterfall, river
Fall Creek Trail	0.25 mile	moderate	Chattooga River
Bull Sluice	0.25 mile	easy	Bull Sluice rapid

Chattooga River - Section IV

Name	Length	difficulty	main attraction
Sutton Hole Trail	0.6 mile	moderate	swimming hole
Woodall Shoals	0.25 mile	moderate	Woodall Shoals rapid
Seven Foot Falls	0.5 mile	mod.- diff.	Seven Foot Falls rapid
Stekoa & Cliff Creek	1.5 miles	moderate	Chattooga River
Long Creek Falls	2.0 miles	moderate	Long Creek Falls
Raven Cliffs Trail	0.8 mile	moderate	Raven Cliffs
Opossum Creek Trail *add'l to Five Falls*	2.0 miles 0.25 mile	moderate difficult	Opossum Creek Falls Five Falls rapids
Camp Creek Trail	0.25 mile	moderate	Chattooga River

Trail lengths listed are one-way to destination unless otherwise noted.

Concerned Organizations

- **Chattooga River Watershed Coalition**
  P.O. Box 2006
  Clayton, GA 30525
  (706) 782-6097, fax 782-6098
  Email: crwc@igc.apc.org

- **Stekoa Creek Water Quality Committee**
  Rt. 3 - Box 3156 E
  Clayton, GA 30525

- **Georgia Forest Watch**
  Route 1, Box 685
  Rabun Gap, GA 30568
  (706) 746-5799

- **Friends of the Mountains**
  P.O. Box 368
  Tallulah Falls, GA 30573
  (706) 754-3310

- **The Georgia Conservancy, Inc.**
  1776 Peachtree Street
  Atlanta, GA 30309
  (404) 876-2900

- **The Nature Conservancy**
  1401 Peachtree Street NE
  Suite 136
  Atlanta, GA 30309
  (404) 873-6946

- **The Wilderness Society**
  1447 Peachtree Street
  Atlanta, GA 30309
  (404) 872-9453

Area State Parks

• Black Rock Mountain State Park

located off Hwy 441 in Mountain City, GA.
P.O. Drawer A
Mountain City, GA 30562
(706) 746-2141

Georgia's highest park, *Black Rock Mountain State Park* features six peaks above 3,000 feet, and offers visitors numerous sublime overlooks. The park headquarters and visitor center is located above a sheer cliff overlooking Clayton, 1,600 feet below. The park is over 1,500 acres, features tent and trailer sites, walk-in camping, rental cottages, playgrounds, picnic shelters, hiking trails and a fishing lake.

• Tallulah Gorge State Park

located on Hwy 441 in Tallulah Falls, GA.
P.O. Box 248
Tallulah Falls, GA 30573
(706) 754-8257

Georgia's newest state park is also one of its most dramatic. The focal point of the park is magnificent Tallulah Gorge, 2 miles long and almost 1,000 feet deep. When complete, the park will encompass over 3,000 acres. The park currently features hiking trails, swimming, tennis, the Jane Hurt Yarn Interpretive Center, camping, a playground, and much more.

• Oconee State Park

12 miles north of Walhalla on Hwy 107.
624 State Park Rd.
Mountain Rest, SC 29664
(864) 638-5353

Situated on a rolling plateau east of the Chattooga, Oconee State Park features numerous recreational opportunities. The park offers campsites, rental cabins, picnic shelters, fishing and boat rental, and hiking trails (including access to the Foothills Trail).

FERN CREEK PRESS
OUTDOOR PUBLISHERS SINCE 1989

The Chattooga Wild and Scenic River, Third edition. Excellent all-around guide to whitewater adventure, hiking and camping on the incomparable Chattooga River. Maps, photos. $10.95 ppd.

Waterfalls of the Southern Appalachians, Third edition. Guide to over 150 magnificent mountain cascades. Complete directions, maps and photos. 160 pages. $10.95 ppd.

Summits of the South Features 25 scenic Southern Appalachian summit adventures, each one delightfully unique. Trips range from short hikes to challenging treks. Something for everyone who wants a roam with a view. Maps, photos. $8.95 ppd.

The Highlands-Cashiers Outdoors Companion Features over 30 natural attractions in the scenic Highlands, NC area. Trails, waterfalls, overlooks. Complete maps and photos. $8.95 ppd.

The Rabun County Outdoors Companion Voted one of the 100 most beautiful counties in *Outdoor* magazine, come explore the mountains, rivers and streams of this beautiful county. Contains recreational information of all kinds. Complete maps and photos. $8.95 ppd

Biking the Trails of Rabun Excellent guide to 30 outstanding mountain biking trips in beautiful Rabun County. Contains helpful information detailing necessary equipment. Map, photos. $10.95 ppd.

coming in 1998... **Great Destinations in the Northeast Georgia Mountains** Guide to the very best natural attractions in the Northeast Georgia mountains. Hikes, overlooks, camping spots, scenic drives. Maps and photos. Due out summer 1998. Please call.

coming in 1998... **The South Carolina Mountains** Describes many of the natural attractions in the often overlooked mountains of northwest South Carolina. Parks, trails, waterfalls, lakes, rivers. Maps and photos. Due out summer 1998. Please call.

We also have a number of regional visitors maps available.

To order books directly, send check or money order to:

Fern Creek Press
P.O. Box 1322 • Clayton, GA 30525
(706) 782-5379

Georgia residents please add 7% sales tax. Thank you.

The Chattooga Wild and Scenic River

CHATTOOGA RIVER ADVENTURES

Raft · Funyak · Whitewater Equipment Rentals

Outfitters Shop • Canoe & Kayak Instruction
Whitewater Equipment Sales • Video • Photography

1-864-647-0365

Custom Guided Lake Canoe & Kayak Tours

Two miles from Chattooga River bridge • Highway 76 in South Carolina
14546-B Long Creek Hwy., Mtn. Rest, SC 29664

LODGING AVAILABLE CLOSE TO HIGHWAY 76 SECTION IV PUT-IN

Where boaters camp at the Chattooga!

LONG CREEK CAMPGROUND

a private campground in the heart of the
CHATTOOGA RIVER Wild and Scenic Area
near the Section IV takeout

864-647-2820
WWW.CDS.NET/LC

turn off US Hwy 76 by **Three Forks Country Store** and follow the signs
2739 Damascus Church Road, Long Creek, SC 29658

CHATTOOGA WILD & SCENIC RIVER

Southeastern Expeditions

For 25 years Southeastern Expeditions has provided professionally guided whitewater rafting trips on the Chattooga River. Full day trips are available both on Sections III and IV while overnight trips (including gear and food) offer a tour of both sections. Whitewater canoe and kayak clinics, group team building seminars and environmental education programs are also available. Southeastern Expeditions - *your Chattooga choice since 1973.*

See 1-800-868-7238

visit our web site at www.southeasternraft.com

The **CHATTOOGA WHITEWATER SHOP** is a leader in the design and development of modern whitewater equipment. We offer a complete selection of equipment for kayaking and rafting. If you are a weekend paddler or an expedition paddler, we can outfit your trip with the right equipment.

- Raft Rentals
  - Inflatable Kayaks
    - Perception Kayaks

business hours 8 A.M. - 6 P.M.

The **CHATTOOGA WHITEWATER SHOP** is located two miles from the Chattooga River on Highway 76 on the South Carolina side. If you are in the area, stop in and have a look around. We will look forward to helping you discover the beauty and excitement of the Chattooga River.

- Equipment Sales • Equipment Rentals
- Canoe & Kayak Clinics • Shuttle Service

14239 Long Creek Highway
Long Creek, SC 29658
(864) 647-9083   fax: (864) 647-4459

Rabun County
"Where Spring spends the Summer"

Chamber of Commerce and Welcome Center

"Discover Hidden Treasures...Old and New"

- Chattooga Wild and Scenic River • Tallulah Gorge
- Fantastic mountain vistas • Three beautiful state parks
- Spectacular mountain lakes • Variety of outdoor recreation
- Excellent lodging and restaurants • Diversity of shopping

(706) 782-4812

Highway 441 • P.O. Box 750CH • Clayton, GA 30525
visit our website at   www.gamountains.com/rabun

Outdoor Adventures

Cathy and Lee Pollard, proprietors

Clothing, Accessories & Supplies for the Outdoorsman in Everyone... Men, Women, and Children

Canoeing • Kayaking • Hiking • Backpacking • Fly Fishing
Nature Gift Shop • Visit our Climbing Wall • Classes Available

864-653-5800

157 Old Greenville Hwy • Clemson, South Carolina

Tallulah Point Overlook

A mountain tradition since the 1920s

Located on Tallulah Gorge
Scenic Loop 15, Tallulah Falls, GA
Open 7 days, April-November
706-754-4318

Come See Us For...

- Nostalgic gifts and souvenirs
- Cider, cold drinks and snacks
- Camping supplies
- Rustic twig furniture by Don Bundrick
- Pottery

After your day on the river, come relax on our covered porch with a nice cold drink and enjoy the best view of Tallulah Gorge!

featuring the best and only FREE roadside view of magnificent Tallulah Gorge!